THE GREEN, GREEN GRASS

Books by the author in the sequence *The Sensual World*

THE GARDENS OF CAMELOT
THE ALTAR IN THE LOFT
THE DRUMS OF MORNING
THE GLITTERING PASTURES
THE NUMBERS CAME
THE LAST OF SPRING
THE PURPLE STREAK
THE WILD HILLS
THE HAPPY HIGHWAYS
THE SOUND OF REVELRY
THE MOON IN MY POCKET
THE LICENTIOUS SOLDIERY
THE BLOOD-RED ISLAND
THE GORGEOUS EAST
THE DOGS OF PEACE
THE LIFE FOR ME
THE VERDICT OF YOU ALL
THE TANGERINE HOUSE
THE QUEST FOR QUIXOTE
THE WINTRY SEA
THE GHOST OF JUNE
THE CAVES OF HERCULES
THE LONG WAY HOME
THE GREEN GREEN GRASS

Supplementary

THE WORLD IS YOUNG
THE MAN IN EUROPE STREET
THE CIRCUS HAS NO HOME

M 1545170

**This book is to be returned on or before
the last date stamped below.**

STORE

06. OCT. 87

28. OCT 87

THE GREEN, GREEN GRASS

Being the twenty-fourth and final book
in the sequence
The Sensual World

by

Rupert Croft-Cooke

W. H. ALLEN · LONDON
A division of Howard & Wyndham Ltd
1977

© *Rupert Croft-Cooke, 1977*

*This book or parts thereof may not
be reproduced without permission in
writing.*

*Printed and bound in Great Britain by
Butler & Tanner Ltd, Frome and London*

*for the publishers, W. H. Allen & Co. Ltd
44 Hill Street, London W1X 8LB*

ISBN 0 491 01836 3

Contents

Contents

One

England, Pubs and Beauty

There are times in the lives of most Englishmen when they realize positively and consciously that they are islanders. So was it on my first travels abroad when the sea passage seemed interminable, or on my many returns to England when having journeyed impatiently across the Continent I went on board at Calais or Ostend to traverse the seasick miles to Dover and Kent and a waiting welcome. Most marked was my sense of a return home in 1973, when having left Germany, which had become odious to me, I arrived in England with no decision about where or even whether to remain in the country I had left twenty years earlier.

Of course there had been numerous visits to London from Spain, Morocco, Cyprus, Italy and Tunisia, and I had never ceased to be English in one or more of the senses in which one belongs to the country, the capital, the county where one was born, but they had been essentially visits, calls on old friends or temporary returns to all I had known in the past. They had never been made with any intention to stay, certainly not to make a home for what might be left of my life. Since going to live abroad in 1954, although I had passed at least a month in every year 'at home', to 'keep in touch' as I probably put it, I had never before contemplated settling in England.

For I had been warned. During my first years in Tangier when visitors from England spoke with increasing bitterness of their homeland, I put it down to their envy of our permissive, picturesque and inexpensive way of life, but as time went on I could not help listening to their grim stories

7

about London and the provinces, especially since our own Tangerine existence grew less pleasant. The high point in their diatribes was usually the exorbitant demands of income tax which would reduce me, and everyone else who was self-employed, to penury. The climate was next in order of unendurability—the sun, according to these informants, had suddenly disappeared from the northern heavens while wind and rain never ceased. Scarcely less to be feared was the crime and violence in the streets, on public vehicles, in pubs and parks—everywhere in fact where a citizen might expect to be unmolested. Football crowds were in a perpetual state of turbulence, while the wars between greasers and skinheads (the rivals of those days) outdid the Wars of the Roses in persistence and cruelty. The expense of keeping oneself alive and under a roof meant the complete abandonment of tobacco and alcohol; viciously bad manners or actual muggings were an everyday experience while a totally incompetent police service was forced to stand by and watch or even add its unpleasantness to that of other offenders. The Health Service cost more and did less than any other in Europe, while housing was a joke in rancidly bad taste.

For public entertainment, we were told, there were only pop festivals which, the dreariness of their music apart, carried the risk of being trodden underfoot by hysterical teenagers trying to reach the pretty boys they idolized, or being arrested for carrying pot or poisoned by 'the hard stuff'. It was impossible to make a living by writing, though if one could set a few bars to imitative music which thus became copyright, one could live luxuriously on the proceeds from a tinkle of melody for the rest of a long life. If one had not secured the domestic service of a wife, one learned to clean floors and wash up plates in a life-long rotation. The only food purchasable within reason came from supermarkets where everything visible was tinned, frozen, precooked, mass-manufactured, dehydrated or advertised on television as 'new' or 'large-sized' or 'special'. You could not easily remain 'self-employed' or inhabit a house that had not the conventional '2 beds, one sit', a kitchen and a garage, considered the appropriate accommodation for a wage-earner and his wife. You enjoyed no casual leisure beyond a strict allowance of fourteen days of poor food and boring companionship in a standard resort on a shivering levante-torn coast of Spain. You must be prepared to be cheeked, if not insulted, by rowdy teenagers or the strident upholders of Women's Lib. Serious crime, we were told, was flagrant and uncontrolled, while the entire countryside was 'ruined' by the spread of factories or bad domestic architecture, and those who admitted having fought in the Second World War were treated with universal contempt, if not hostility. It was all rather like the period immediately after that war except that there were now few shortages for those whose incomes were ensured by the sacrifices of others.

Yet these warnings meant little to me, conditioned as I had been all the years of my life to dealing with them, or others like them. Income tax was not a menace since I did not earn enough to make it payable. Of the weather I had few fears, having lived in Ireland, and as for the expense of everything—I had been for the last year in Germany where a cup of coffee in a common café cost a pound. I could dismiss most of the other threats, so that once having resolved to live in England, I was content to rely on that peculiar form of good luck which is the only kind to smile on me, luck in finding a home and someone to carry out such domestic labour as I needed. England would provide a background which I felt was the right one for me and friendships which even in my seventies I found easy to make. It would be the most daring move I had undertaken, wherever I had gone before, and to settle in my own country would take more courage and spirit of adventure than when I had gone to strange foreign places in Asia, Africa and South America.

'You know nothing of England,' said one of those candid friends who do not 'mince words'—whatever that means. 'Spending a week or two here in every year in the home of

Patrick Kinross in Little Venice, or being given theatre seats for new shows by Peter Daubeny, or invited down to Buscot by Gavin Faringdon, what do you expect to know of everyday life from these? You won't be able to stand it after a couple of months. So for God's sake don't burn your boats in North Africa because you'll be crying to go back before the first winter comes.' I was obstinately determined to do nothing of the sort, and as I left Cologne, which had been my last stopping-place abroad, and began the crossing from Ostend to Dover I counted such blessings as were mine in anticipation, including the greatest of them all, the Indian secretary, friend, adopted son or younger brother who had stood by me with Kiplingesque reliability for thirty-odd years, in times of real penury and most other ills the flesh is heir to. He was with me as we came into Dover, though I had to leave him to satisfy the immigration officials, confident that though he was very obviously not English they would not treat him with the insolent arrogance of their Hitler-bred counterparts in the Germany we had just left.

In that I was right. I had only just taken places in the waiting London train when Joseph appeared smiling, with an obliging Cook's man carrying his luggage. He had been given three months to stay in England. 'Time enough,' said the genial immigration officer, 'to make arrangements if you want to stay longer.'

So far, so good. When he had first elected to come with me to England at the end of the last war, he had travelled far more comfortably third-class on a liner running from Bombay to Southampton than I had as an officer on a troop-ship bound for Liverpool, and had been accepted in England with a warmer welcome as a British Empire citizen than I had received as a soldier due for release after four years overseas and six in the Army. Neither he nor I expected similar treatment now that factories and railways were colourfully staffed, and houses occupied by Asians, West Indians and Africans drawn from their natural habitat by promises of higher wages; dark men who shivered and grumbled in a climate which they found all but unbearable. For Joseph, who had spent nine years in England before we had left it for the Mediterranean, the climate had no terrors and indeed he had always been more homesick for London (though perhaps in a less familiar and indigenous sense) than I had during our years of foreign residence. He genuinely loved the English, not as a foreigner who had known them as rulers of his country, but as friends or, perhaps one might say more dialectically, as co-Aryans. So he was not surprised to be received with kindly courtesy by the British immigration officers.

But when the Kentish fields and woods began to swim by the train windows, I had thoughts only for these. At one point in the journey between Dover and London I had been familiar with the railway seen from the road, that was as it went on its way up to Town approaching Headcorn and passing near the Bell at Smarden, the pub among all the familiar ones of Kent which had been 'my own'. It stood a few yards from Smarden Grange in which my father had died and I had afterwards lived. My brother and I had worn a footpath through the plum orchards which separated pub and house, and The Bell remained alive in many memories. It was to The Bell that I had guided the Rosaires with their circus wagons when the outbreak of war had stopped their performances; The Bell near which my own gypsy wagon had stood before I had started on my journey with Ted Scamp; The Bell in which I had known the brothers Homewood of a vanished generation and the lovable eccentric John Torr, all from scenes in the rustic pantomime of my life before I had joined the Army, all figures now vanished but memorable still.

The Bell was not visible from the train windows but as we rumbled across the Weald of Kent I knew that from wherever I should settle in England I would return to Smarden and enliven my mind with its associations. Why else indeed had I left the sunlight of the Mediterranean and come to England if it was not to visit such beloved places as this?

There were other pubs where I had talked and drunk beer and played darts in times past, not hotels or restaurants or cafés or tea-houses or even inns, but *pubs* in which I had felt at home, sometimes for many evenings or even years. Several of them were in Kent, for I had been loyal to my county during what years I had spent in England and I knew every square mile of it, and its pubs had been my most familiar stamping grounds. The Bull at Wrotham to which I had come nightly during the year or two I had occupied that thatched and whitewalled cottage which overlooked the crossroads on the way to London, where I had played darts with Li'nel, Alf and Old Goble and gone after closing time to a natural bathing-pool unknown to outsiders and formed by a deep disused quarry a mile from the road.

In a village where there is more than one pub, every man has his own. 'I use The King's Head', 'I go to The Wheatsheaf', and so on, and these habits once formed continue till some incident, some disagreement or perhaps an unaccountable change of mood dictates a new affiliation. 'I don't go to The Feathers any more, not after What Was Said', 'I've taken to The Chequers lately. They've got New People there', and so on. I had myself undergone one of these changes of outlook and abandoned the habit of 'using' The Rose and Crown. This was because the landlord was a retired manservant who had spent his life in the household of a rich industrialist. It had made him both servile and pretentious, smarmy yet what my father called a 'good-as-you-are kind of fellow', and I had taken a dislike to him and removed my custom—I might almost say my allegiance— to The Bull.

The Bull at Wrotham today, I believe, is an important hostelry, qualifying for stars in lists of hotels and restaurants published by competing agencies. Then, except at weekends during the summer months, it was a village pub, an ancient house with uneven flooring and dark little rooms with a private bar within the house, and across the carriageway a public bar in what had once been the stables. This last was my nightly resort.

12

At weekends The Bull changed its character, for its large stable-yard became a parking place for what were then called char-à-bancs or 'sharries' and have now been undeservedly dignified with the name 'coaches'. Wrotham was a convenient stopping-place for these on their journeys from London to the coast and even more on their rowdy return journeys from the coast to London, and extra bars were opened up in the yard to serve the sun-smitten people who came tumbling out of them. London workers had learned none of the sophistications of today, and a weekend or even a day by the sea with plenty of beer and a good old singsong on the way back was for most of them a summer holiday, and the rest of their free week, if they got one, was spent at home or on the allotment.

Then it was good to see them. There were inhabitants of Wrotham, particularly the owners of the fine old house with a walled garden adjoining The Bull yard, who objected to these weekly saturnalia, but I was not among them. The bawling of old songs, the music and action of *Knees Up, Mother Brown*, the quick change of mood to lachrymose ballads, the occasional fights, the raw, loud, reeling turbulence of it delighted me, and my cottage, quiet among its trees, was a full quarter of a mile away.

Earlier than that, in the 1920s when my parents lived on the 'new estate' of bungalows called New Barn and I had been given a disused Army hut (of the First World War) in which to live and write, I remember slipping away to visit a rather sordid little pub called The Green Man at Longfield Hill between New Barn and Meopham, famous for its permissive opening hours and its entertainment of four lively brothers, sons of a farmer named Woodward. They had a reputation for notable practical joking and devil-may-care eccentricity. I met all of them at different times in The Green Man, and the oldest, Don Woodward, used to lend me a horse and come for long rides with me far away from the bungalows and neatly hedged roads of New Barn. I had not then learned to play darts, and our evenings were spent in anecdotes or talk of cricket and racing—a welcome change

13

for me after a day's concentration on writing. The bars were ill-lit and the beer lifeless but the talk among the Woodward brothers did not lack incident or spirit and has left legends which I have heard repeated in recent times. How, when they were refused drink after hours at a pub in Harvell, they had raised terror by standing outside and shouting: 'We'll huff and we'll puff and we'll blow the house down!' Or how, unable to pass a Maidstone District bus in a narrow lane, they drove it in reverse and full of passengers, back to the main road. I have always loved rebels, particularly when they are motivated by nothing but mischief and humour, and I admired all four brothers in those long ago days.

Earlier still, when I had been employed to teach preparatory schoolboys at the New Beacon, Sevenoaks, The Royal Oak was the pub of my choice since it was at the top of a narrow lane which led to the High Street. Of the proprietor, an ex-Army caterer named Robinson, or his circle of customers, respectable local tradesmen, I can only wonder that they put up with me, an egocentric boy of eighteen who sat on the floor near the fire and quoted Swinburne and consulted them about my forthcoming visit by motorbike to Kipling at Burwash, and gave them a full account of it on my return.

Even earlier than that, in the days of my youngest childhood, a mere picture remains in my mind of a pub scene which might have been by an eighteenth-century watercolour artist. My beloved Ninna had taken me, aged three or four, by an unfamiliar road near Lindfield in Sussex, where we lived. I remember the housefront of a small-windowed pub which stood back from the road, and when I came to read Wells's *Mr Polly* I saw that the Potwell Inn exactly accorded with this memory. As Ninna and I went by, keeping to the left of the road, we saw that a wagon with two horses stood outside the public bar, peaceful until a din arose at the door and the driver of the wagon, a bearded man wearing a smock and gaiters, was ejected by the landlord and unsteadily climbed to the seat of the wagon and took up the reins to move off. Ninna clutched my hand firmly but I was watching that startling scene and can remember it still seventy years later.

No such unseemly events took place outside The White Hart in Chipstead, to which enchanted village on the Surrey Downs we moved next, though many carts and drays pulled up before it as I passed with my sister and our governess in the years before the First World War. The landlord was a good citizen who worked with my father to promote the village flower-show, and I resolved as I thought of it that I would revisit Chipstead and do what I had never been permitted to do as a little boy, peep into the mysterious interior of the place with the name which had aroused my childish curiosity (what *was* a White Hart?).

A year or two later, but still before the outbreak of the First World War, I actually entered a bar when I had walked across the then unpopulated Downs from Seaford, where we had gone for our summer holidays, to Alfriston, a distance which I now see from the AA Handbook is four miles, though it seemed farther then. I was with my father alone and his decision to take me was made at the last moment and against the advice of my mother. This gave the excursion beside my father the air of a slightly illicit adventure, highly enjoyable to me. I do not remember the name of the pub, which had blackened beams and old furniture, but I remember my father drinking a pint of beer and giving me a ginger beer for our respective thirsts. And then in a room upstairs there was roast beef and gooseberry tart and cream, and I strode proudly back to Seaford, keeping pace with my portly father's longer steps. I returned to Alfriston with my friend John Hitchcock some years later and heard in the public bar of a more modest pub the actual singing (not a recreated folksy revival) of an eighteenth—or was it seventeenth-century?—country song with the chorus of 'They call I Buttercup Joe'.

The first bar in which I ever ordered a drink was that of the Station Buffet at Eastbourne when I used to wait for my father from his London train on most evenings. It was

Port that I drank with a good friend of those days whose name was Tom Hole, a great-nephew of Dean Hole whose *Book About Roses* changed the face of English horticulture. Tom soon advanced to beer, but a glass of port 'drawn from the wood' at sixpence was my furthest venture. It was with my parents that I first drank in an inn when they had come down all the way from Eastbourne to Wellington, Shropshire, and had taken me, with my friends Bowen and Hepper, two Yorkshiremen, and Oswald Horrax, the school-master I liked best, to The Charlton Arms for lunch.

The Rose and Crown at Tonbridge stood in a similar re-lation to the School, and its restaurant was crowded by parents giving their Tonbridgian sons glorious meals to relieve the paucity of the wartime catering in most of the Houses. I remember it best for the traditional scene on Skinners' Day, when the Master of the Skinners' Company came out on the crested balcony above the front entrance and was cheered by the whole school, dripping from their immersion, not in the school swimming bath but by a long-standing tradition in the Medway itself. If Tonbridge had not become a cranky co-educational, or comprehensive, or experimental school, I would go down again to the town, I resolved, and revive even more poignant memories than those of Shropshire.

But I had not yet finished with Kent in this imaginary gazetteer of pubs. One of the most familiar remained to recall—The Bull at Rochester, which even to Dickensians could not mean much more than it meant to me. The char-acters whom my brother and I met in the bar when we came to it nightly from our bookshop a few doors down the High Street were not Pickwickian, but with a childish and malicious enjoyment I clumsily caricatured them all in my second novel *Give Him the Earth* (1930) in which the heroine became a barmaid there.

'As the days went by she began to know them. Most of them, it seemed, were "regulars" – neighbouring shop-keepers and local clerks, Greycastrians who made this

particular bar their rendezvous. There was the tobac-
conist, a sharp-featured man who called her Miss and
invited her to have a spot with him; the stertorous
keeper of a temperance hotel who did not; a couple of
young insurance agents, one of whom was over-dressed
and unpopular because he occasionally left the accepted
channels of conversation to describe his dreams, which
were prolific; the other with the reputation of a "sheik"
and a soft voice that came straying out of his pleasant,
rather baby face. There was a tedious old solicitor who
wore an ill-fitting wig, and tried to make her buy a copy
of his *History of Greycaster* for fifteen shillings, and a
marauding young solicitor who was rapidly securing his
practice. There was a ginger-pated hairdresser who threw
his arm round everyone and called them "dear boy",
and the dipsomaniac manager of a local factory. There
was an asthmatic ass who had been left shares in the same
concern, and a number of minor employees of it who
followed their leader. There was a couple of young
brothers who kept a bookshop, the elder freckled, large-
headed, long-nosed, the younger sallow and inquisitive,
both excitingly dressed, and greatly disliked by the
"regulars". There was a perspiring official from the town
hall opposite, and the manager of an ice-cream concern
who had been in China and could not forget it. There
was a corn-haired car salesman who was always growing
moustaches and shaving them off again, and a naval
officer who could not grow one at all. And so on.'

Other pubs in England belonged to other periods in the
past, and some of them I hoped to see again. All those in
Ticehurst, in which village of two thousand inhabitants
there were three flourishing pubs and an equally flourishing
lunatic asylum. The landlords of all these risked the renewal
of their licences by supporting me in the vicious attack
which the local police made on me, and in which the so-called
'gentry' of the place heartily joined.

I must cross almost the whole length of the county to

find the village of Denton in what was then one of the loneliest stretches of country in Kent, between Canterbury and Birchington. I have heard lewd tales of its present-day transformation, with coalfields and airports near it, but then it was a small, uncrowded village of old houses and one pub. If that pub seen years before in Lindfield reminded me of the Potwell Inn in *Mr Polly*, then the aptly named Mrs Billows closely resembled its landlady. I had never returned to it after hurrying away at the time to the Switzerland I described in *Cosmopolis* and *The White Mountain*, but I determined to do so now that I should have time to visit all the old pubs of my acquaintance in Kent.

Nor were the pubs familiar to me in pre-war days limited to Kent and Sussex. The richest in gypsies at the time of pea-picking and later of the Horse Fair was The Star at Pershore from which I joined the Army in 1940, and in which I learned the shouted choruses of the songs loved by Romanies and saw in the yard some violent fights. True, I used to breakfast at The Angel, a grander pub altogether, but The Star was my spiritual home. There were other pubs I remembered patronizing in passing—a fine one at Diss in Norfolk, where the landlady always added in parenthesis to her husband's name 'Eton and Balliol'; another found at Poolewe on a drive through the Highlands with my friend John Hitchcock, where we witnessed a recruiting sergeant obtaining a signature from an intoxicated recruit, a scene like one in the days of the Press-gang a century earlier. There was another which I cannot identify near Padstow in Cornwall when I stayed there; it had a low ceiling in the bar-parlour, and was lit by a paraffin lamp to show one what looked like the Phoenician cap of a French revolutionary on the head of one old fisherman. Nor must I forget the Gloucestershire pubs in which I played darts, also by lamplight, where curved settles stood round the fire in which pokers were heated to mull both ale and cider.

During the war in the few months I remained in the Army in England and Scotland, before finding more exotic bars in the East and Africa, there were several pubs I remember fondly. The Southgate at Winchester, near King Alfred's College which was our training centre in 1940, The Green Dragon in Chester in which I was billeted, and that most generous of all pubs, The Queen's Head at Kelso where the proprietress, the bountiful Mrs Easson, allowed me to billet myself when I was on detachment to the Marines. I have always wanted to return to this pub in which at the time of Pearl Harbour I was allowed to wear civilian clothes and eat salmon fresh from the Tweed, and drive about in Mrs Easson's car with my dearest friend Stewart Hamilton, a stocky Irishman from Tyrone, who died before he might have been dragged into the wretched maelstrom of his native Northern Ireland, the only man for whom (though he was a Protestant) I pray 'God Rest His Soul'.

In the years since the war I shall recall only the Fitzroy tavern and its proprietors Annie and Charles Allchild, a pub with great traditions, literary, dramatic, political and in a strange way, social. I had heard later that its licensees had left it and taken with them their distinctive circle, their famous collection of First World War posters, and the little drip tap installed in the nineties for adding water to absinthe. I knew that this most characterful pub was feature-less now, a respectable drinking-place like any other in London, with none of its old vivacity and panache, and I knew this was one place I should never revisit though I had not lost the friendship of Annie and Charlie Allchild.

I have many times attempted to explain to foreigners what exactly is an English pub, and have always failed. I fail now, steering away from the folksy descriptions from brewers' advertising agents and sentimentalists of the past.

Pubs, honest-to-goodness pubs were ahead of me now that I was returning to England. It seemed to me, thinking of them, that most of the years between 1925 and 1940, that is from my twenty-second to thirty-seventh years, had been spent either abroad or in English pubs. Not that I was a heavy drinker. I drank beer in those days and played darts, often from opening time till closing time, the stake on each game against my rustic competitors being strictly 'half a pint of bitter' (fourpence ha'penny then) and 'one for the scorer', while if you were fanciful or extravagant enough to want something else you 'paid the difference'.

Were they wasted, those mulled and happy hours in Kent, Gloucestershire and elsewhere, hours of increasing proficiency at the game, hours of inerudite but warm companionship? I knew they were not. They taught me not only to start on the double-eighteen, score on the treble-twenty and finish on the double-sixteen (because it split down evenly) but something far more important—to know and sympathize with, and sometimes help the underpaid working men of those days. If they were married they could not come to the pub more than on one evening a week and their hours there were precious to them, while if they were still single they might turn up more regularly, but a game of darts was a vital matter for them since they never played unless they had the money to stand the winner a drink, and a game won meant they could play again.

I must have known scores of them, playing by lamplight in The Puesdown Inn or The Frog Mill near my home in the Cotswolds, or at The Bull at Wrotham or at pubs scattered about the counties I travelled. I remember no meanness, no sullenness, no hostility in all those years in pubs. I was proud of their acceptance of me as one of themselves and believed myself more genuinely a socialist in that acceptance than all the Oxbridge graduates who belonged to the Labour Party or the Left Book Club. There was no pretence about my enjoyment of pubs; I loved them for themselves and the men (and very occasionally women) I met in them. I was proud of my darts—for though I had tried to participate in almost all sports and games, rugby, football, tennis, cricket, riding, ski-ing and even polo in Argentina and golf in Shropshire, I had never become even a moderately successful player at any game until I discovered the delightful pastime of darts. All my four brothers were athletes of one kind or another and Laurie had a half-blue for cross-country running; all of them were able to defeat me at every sport we tried until the lucky day when I discovered that by some chance or curious skill I could throw darts in a way not only to win against them all, but to win *beer*. My friends Barton Wills and John Hitchcock were brilliant runners and cricketers respectively but they 'couldn't touch' me, as the expression goes, at darts.

But it was not only the game that I enjoyed, it was the warmth and laughter on ugly winter nights when in the country there was nothing to do but go to a pub and 'try to get on the board'. The hours passed easily till closing time while a few coarse jokes were exchanged and a few confidences were whispered.

Always when I had been abroad before the war the pubs were waiting for me and they were now, please God, as I came home.

Two

Amira Court

As the train came into London I faced more immediate questions. I was to stay in the house of Patrick Kinross who had given me refuge on so many occasions in the last twenty years, and Joseph was to go to Coventry (in the literal and not the metaphorical sense) where he would stay in the home of one of the few people whose friendship we shared. I had known Donald Ebrahim since I had come out of the Army in 1946. He was the son of a Pakistani Muslim who had been trained in medicine in England, had indeed stayed at my home in Ticehurst while taking his final exams. He was now a popular G.P. who devoted much of his time to psychiatry and hypno-therapy. He had invited Joseph to stay in his big house on the outskirts of Coventry while I was looking for a home in which we could settle.

This, I was warned by friends everywhere, would be difficult if not impossible in London and scarcely less so in the provinces. But once again I was determined to trust in my particular form of luck and started to search, as we are told in heart-breaking stories 'young married couples' (apparently the most invariably disappointed species of house-seekers) did so pointlessly. Discarding a small furnished house in a slum near King's Cross station which the kindly owner offered me, in preference, she said, to letting it to an American who would pay much more than the £25 a week it would cost me, I impulsively abandoned London altogether and lowered my sights to the country. Friends were helpful and I accepted Robin Maugham's invitation to Brighton to 'look round', but found that furnished accommodation at monstrous prices was the only possibility, and that in small terraced houses on the outskirts, smelling of gas mains and crowded with shabby Victorian furniture, the previous inhabitants had apparently lived without fresh air or tap-water for a century. There were also flats in lofty Regency buildings, with pretentious furniture, twelve-foot high windows and intimidating conditions under which they could be let, to childless couples only, for short periods at £40 a week.

I next appealed to John Hitchcock who himself had a converted Elizabethan house and grounds with a swimming-pool to suit his status as a magnate in the nickel industry. We decided that Folkestone was the likeliest place in Kent, since Joseph was unhappy in rural surroundings and needed shops and cinemas, while I could take any city which had the open country within its reach. But Folkestone, it seemed, had shrunk since I had last driven through, and as far as I could gather had only one busy shopping street and suburbs of hideous houses. A Cinque Port, it had a formidable history and had been a popular watering-place in Victorian times, but for me it could not escape the impression of a run-down resort, neither old and picturesque nor yet modern and lively enough to have attractions either way. An inoffensively furnished flat was to let at a reasonable price, but it was on the fifth floor, which put it out of the question for me since I had suffered a heart attack in Tunis three years before.

So it was back to London to hear more advice from good friends that I should take whatever I could get in these difficult times of 1973, that since there could be no mortgage for me at my age and unfurnished flats were unobtainable, the most I could hope for was an expensive furnished flat and *that* out of London. Everyone houseless faced this problem, I was told. Hadn't I been warned that this was the state of things in England? Why on earth had I come home? Or equally comfortlessly, why had I *not* come a few years ago? As for believing that I should eventually find something (*not* what I wanted of course, the idea belonged to the world of fantasy and should be dropped forthwith), well the idea was not quite unthinkable. Did I think I was in some way privileged to expect to succeed where no one ever did? I did not, but I went on looking.

During my young manhood there was a mode for inverted snobbery, and popular rhymesters of the period, Auden, Spender *et alia,* not only called themselves poets but 'Left-Wing Poets' to boot. The wearing of tattered jeans came later, but reporting the so-called anti-Fascist wars (in Spain and China) was all the go until our own hideous war broke out.

For me it was not enough to counter this inverted snobbery by claiming working-class origins, as so many writers did, and picturing an impressionistic childhood spent in a miner's cottage or a Liverpool slum—I needed more aggressive variants and reminded readers and listeners that I was the very type and personification of the middle class (just then more unpopular and derided than even aristocrats). I was everything held in contempt by the Left—the son of a member of the London Stock Exchange who commuted daily from the Home Counties and made tidy little late Victorian gardens, and fumed at 'Socialist beasts'. He frequently used the term 'common' for people whom he considered slightly inferior to himself in the social scale, and as a father insisted on his children's respect for his own values. This gave an altogether unjust picture of my father, who liked and respected workers in all trades and occupations, and as for Fascism or Nazism, he counted as his closest friends members of the Jewish faith and race with whom he 'did business' and who were frequent visitors to our homes. Particularly, what he called (with how much accuracy I do not know) Orthodox Jews who, he maintained, had a higher degree of honour and honesty than others. Their sons became my friends in childhood and have remained so all my life. The Lazarus family in most of its many branches were my familiars and George Lazarus (who has now become its tribal chief, I am told) was sent to the same preparatory school as I was. Rafe Carvalho, of particular eminence in Jewish society, used to spend summer holidays with us on the Norfolk Broads, and I still remember his son Ian, my contemporary, as a young man—intelligent, humorous and shrewd. There were many others, and my childhood would have been a duller time without them.

I exclude Louis Golding from these partisan recollections because he seemed to me to want to run with the hare and hunt with the hounds of Jewry, using his race as 'copy' for his books but indifferent to the dearest tenets of its creed.

All this as prelude to the fact that at this time—July, 1973—I had a particular friend in that select company of London Jewish families which stand out from the humdrum British middle classes as they have stood out for centuries, artists, politicians, financiers and aristocrats of their race. His name was Alan Blond; he was a cousin to Anthony Blond, the publisher, but it would take a skilled genealogist to trace his relationship to all the distinguished members of his kin. Together in Tangier we had discovered the delights of the game so stupidly misnamed 'Scrabble' and played it sometimes late into the night. Together we had planned to issue a periodical (as I had done fifty years ago in Buenos Aires) and together we had motored from Algeciras to London, and to many remote places in Morocco itself. He had discriminating taste and humour and we had laughed at the same things and people.

It was at 'this point of time', in the odious cliché beloved of television spielers, that Alan, who had returned to England, wrote to me from the house he had bought in the New Forest and suggested that I should come down and stay to 'view the prospect o'er', and particularly—since he knew that Joseph was a metropolitan—the town of Bournemouth.

Now Bournemouth was notable to me for several reasons. After the Victorian wedding of my father and mother in 1895—an event which I was fond of picturing in all its conventional details—it was at the Royal Bath Hotel in Bournemouth that they had spent their honeymoon. My younger brother had done the same after his wedding in

1938, and his son, my nephew Derek, had followed what had become a family tradition after the Second World War. This meant nothing but an amusing coincidence to me, but in the 1920s there had been a small broadcasting station in Bournemouth and on several occasions I had gone down there to broadcast at two guineas a time. The studio was in a busy street and the noise of traffic was excluded only by windows. How I came to this I cannot remember but it was no son of my father who paid seventeen shillings return third-class and seven and six for bed and breakfast in a commercial hotel near the station, spending the best part of two days on the venture for a fee rather smaller than those at Savoy Hill. I remembered the occasion in *The Numbers Came*:

'On the journey down I fell into one of those conversations between strangers which in England are rare but when they happen are often surprisingly artless and expressive, perhaps because someone who will never be seen again is like a priest in a confessional. There were three people with me in the compartment, each travelling alone, a grey-haired man smoking a pipe, a big beefy fellow not much older than I, and a thin middle-aged woman with spectacles who remained apparently absorbed in her book.

'The beefy man started it. I had a pile of new books to review for *G.K.'s Weekly* and was turning these over and reading here and there. (Among them I remember was a strangely beautiful and vivid book about Edward Thomas written anonymously by his widow.) The beefy man asked me some question about them which, I expect, I was only too ready to answer. I was twenty-two, a writer, I had these books to review, I was going to Bournemouth to broadcast. In return he told me that he was just back from Burma and was returning there after his leave. He had recently been promoted in the civil service or the police. When he began to talk about the country and the people, there was an emotional vibration in his voice. He had learned the language and "quite settled down" out there. He hoped to get married while on leave but he had told his fiancée that Work Came First. "Oh yes," he repeated, as though this was the boldest thing he had ever said, as well it may have been, "you have to get that straight. In a country like Burma where there is so much to do, work comes first. Otherwise you'd be letting them down. My fiancée understands that. I want to get on, out there. There's a tremendous future in the service. They need us, you see."

'As we talked the woman continued to read her book and the elderly man to smoke and stare out of the window. But presently we were interrupted. The man removed his pipe and said, "I'm going abroad, too."

'The beefy one was polite, called him "Sir" and asked chattily where he was going. "I'm going round the world," said the older man in a quiet sad voice, and stared out of the window again. The beefy young man looked at me and wanted to wink. He could think of nothing to say. But he did not need to answer. "Yes," said the grey-haired man. "I've always meant to do it, when I retire. Right round the world. I'm going next week. I retired from business last month. Passage booked. India, China, Japan, America. I shall take a year to do it." "And after that, sir?" asked the beefy young man, good-humoured but a trifle embarrassed. The older man blinked at him. "After that?" he asked as if in perplexity. "Oh, I don't know. It doesn't matter." How awful, I was thinking, how awful it must be to be old. "It doesn't matter." Incredible that anyone should talk like that. But the beefy young man was full of curiosity and common sense. "You can't say that, sir," he smiled. "Why, you're . . ." "It doesn't matter," repeated the other absently. "Ceylon I want to see particularly. And Bali. I've read a lot about Bali. I've been waiting for this, you know."

'The journey was nearly over before the woman spoke. Then she dismissed the old man's plans, or perhaps it was the plans of all three of us, or of all men, or of all mankind. She spoke a single word to the compartment at large, she spoke clearly and forcefully before returning to her book. "Ridiculous," she said.'

Rather a pale piece of reminiscence to draw one down to Bournemouth nearly half a century later but it served, particularly backed by Alan Blond's invitation. So, with nowhere but a patch of Brighton, some streets in Folkestone and an unlikeable region of Kilburn dismissed as alternatives, I set out for the New Forest.

Like the woodcutters' cottages in fairy stories, Alan's house was deep in the forest and from its windows only trees and stunted woodlands between them were visible. This gave a kind of enchantment to it—enchantment recalling Tennyson with his Merlin and Lady of the Lake or Maurice Hewlett with his *Forest Lovers*. When I woke in the small hours on my first night there, this was perceptible in the view from my bedroom window, moonlit spaces of grass and shadowy trees swaying reproachfully to one another. There was a silence, not complete but erratic, made by the rustling of the leaves disturbed by breezes or, as I felt while I stood aware of its restlessness, by creatures of the forest. It was an expectant silence, not a comatose one, and presently I realized what it expected, for a nightingale's song, clear and powerful, came from the darkness. A devout reader of W. H. Hudson ever since Jack Squire had told me to read *El Ombú* before leaving for South America, I knew then what Hudson meant in *Hampshire Days* when he wrote of the New Forest.

I had never been in the New Forest before—certainly not in the moonlight and breathlessness of an early autumn night, and I was drawn to it more surely and willingly than I had been attracted to the Kentish woods of years ago. There was something miraculous about this place, surviving by a life-force of its own while bleating motor-roads crisscrossed it and townspeople noisily picnicked in its clearings and a great motor museum, with attendant cafés and sightseers, filled its one-time monastic premises. There was something memorable in its very name since it had not been 'new' in a literal sense for two thousand years or more and defied many modern outrages.

But it was not for me. I should, like any townsman, come here to walk and explore and appreciate, but to live in this eerie and beautiful place would be disastrous. I had to face the fact that in spite of my early upbringing I was a townsman and needed the so-called amenities of a town as much as Joseph did. So I gratefully took my place in Alan's car to drive into Bournemouth, armed with local newspapers, to see what possibilities, if any, offered themselves.

At first it was disappointing. The seaside towns on the South Coast I remembered from adolescence: Eastbourne, Hastings, Brighton, Margate, Bexhill and the rest all had recognizable features and people familiar to the visitor, whether they were spoken of by their popular names or whether they had more refined adjuncts called St Leonards, Hove, or Cliftonville, which were invariably used by their insistently pretentious residents. They were peopled with what my father called 'decent-class people' who came into the town to do their shopping, ladies with the status symbol of a fur coat and young boys with ties proclaiming their public school, or older men with flannels and blazers who smoked pipes. These had evidently disappeared from Bournemouth, and though I did not regret this and was delighted to see youths with original clothes and untamed hair, yet I found it hard to be reconciled to the loud Brummagem voices, the lewdly dressed young women dragged along by the encircling arms of sweaty oafs with high heels. I recognized that they, as they are persistently told in print, had every right to be there, that they in my father's favourite term were 'as good as you are', that the world had spun on a time or two (as makers of television commercials say), and when it came to Bournemouth, once the most exclusive of watering-places, I could not help regretting the ladies who changed their books at Boots Lending Library, the public schoolboys on holiday who arranged tennis matches in the parks, and the young ladies who had recently 'put their hair up'. Nor do I believe that this made me a fuddy-duddy or a snob. Most middle-class folk, if they dared to speak the truth in modern life, would prefer to meet their own kind in public places rather than even the worthiest of shrieking mums who are usually richer than they are, and most middle-class parents would like to bring up their children speaking with some pretence to a decent accent rather than that of an Australian television comedian or an aggressive scouse. But the people who crowded the footpaths of Bournemouth were a cheerful and friendly crowd and, as I found out in the time ahead, noticeably more courteous and considerate than the passers-by in other European countries I had known, and most surprising of all *younger*. The old gentlemen in retirement, the old ladies wrapped in comforting if unassuming mink, seemed to have disappeared or, in one sense or another, gone underground and left their cheerful juniors to monopolize the scene, heavily bearded though the youths might be and transvestite though the girls.

The first of two furnished flats we had to view was discovered in the endless maze of residential streets far from the shopping centre or the sea. It contained the necessary number of rooms and was not actually offensively furnished but I could see no reason for wanting to live in it, or wanting to live at all if I should be forced to occupy it, and I moved on to the next possibility. This, too, was a furnished flat at a rent far higher than I had ever paid before, but it was so very much what I wanted that my spirits rose at once. It was a few hundred yards from The Square, the shopping centre, the very focus of Bournemouth, round which theatres, cinemas, department stores and public gardens were set in a careful pattern, and yet it was in a street which escaped the uniformity of the rows of villas and boarding-houses elsewhere in the town. It was on the ground floor of a white-painted block three storeys high and it had a paved patio in front of it, dividing this from the road fifteen feet below it by a high bank of rhododendrons. It had been furnished not, it seemed, for temporary occupation by holiday-makers but in reasonably fair taste, with thick all-over carpets and ivory white walls. It had two bedrooms with two beds each, an adequate kitchen and a small but sufficient bathroom. Above all, it was a cheerful flat, one in which I knew at once (after recent experiences in eight countries described in *The Long Way Home*) that I could live and be happy and write, and about which I knew with certainty that Joseph would feel the same. The sun beat down on the gaily-coloured Dutch blinds and the noise of the traffic was deadened by the fact that the flat stood so far above the road.

But . . . No. It's all right. I am not going to attempt to give the reader who may have suffered the disappointment of house-hunting, a kind of artificial suspense about this. The agent said someone else had yet to give his references and if the arrangement fell through he would let me know by telephone in London. So I agreed to sign a lease if I could have the flat, and there the matter stood till punctually on the Tuesday following when I had returned to Little Venice, he telephoned and agreed, saying he would draw up a lease at once.

So my luck had held once again.

There were of course doubts in the days following. I had not moved through eight countries in North Africa and Europe in search of a home without fears of disappointment now. I had only been in the flat five minutes or so; could it really be so convenient and livable as I remembered it? The rooms were small; too small for the few odds and ends I had kept which were arriving from Germany at any minute? Was it really as gay and cheerful and free from building-estate sameness with its fellows as I remembered it now? Perhaps I had made a ghastly mistake? I had spent so much time in the last few years in looking for a home that perhaps I had become obsessed with a subject too selfish and unworthy of a man's whole consideration, so that I might have misjudged the situation which—as adults said to me in childhood—would serve me right. At all events it was too late now. I had agreed to sign a lease; Joseph was arriving next day and the furniture the day after, and I had given up the room in Little Venice which my friend had so kindly let me use. So there it was—*alea jacta est*. On a Friday morning during early July I sat with Joseph on one of the convenient trains which left Waterloo for Bournemouth at hourly intervals—fast and slow trains alternately. By lunch-time that day all doubts about the wisdom of the move were gone and up till now, three years later, they have never been at all alarmingly re-awakened.

That demands an explanation. Here was a conventional two-bedroomed flat on the ground floor of an unexceptional block of similar ones in a seaside town known for its gentility, formality and popularity among Midland folk seeking retirement, a flat furnished with the standardized necessities of modern housekeeping, a flat, in a word, like many other pleasant sets of rooms provided with the accepted conveniences for two people. Yet, after living at much lower cost in many exotic houses in sunny climates, I knew that this, Number 4, Amira Court, Bourne Avenue, Bournemouth, was exactly the home I wanted, perhaps even the home which consciously or unconsciously I had wanted for most of my life. And the same certainty was Joseph's, though he had been born in the tropics and had little experience of provincial English life.

It had for me many 'advantages', as estate agents call such dubious promises as proximity to a Baptist chapel or a golf-course, or winding paths to the front door, or double-glazed windows. Perhaps the 'advantages' I sought would have been no more desirable in most people's eyes than these, but at least I had earned knowledge of them through many, sometimes disappointing, experiences. This flat had, if not a 'view', at least a pleasant outlook, for under its windows at thirty yards or so distance were a number of tennis courts where tanned and handsome young men, stripped to the waist, disported themselves, and lovely (at this distance anyway) girls showed as much as was considered decent of sun-tanned skin. Their shouts were scarcely audible from my patio but they moved well in the ballet-like skills of the game. Behind the tennis courts were enormous conifers quite concealing tall Victorian houses, and the gardens had been planted with a splendid collection of unusual shrubs. There was no single aspect which was offensive or even drab. For this, stretching upstream and down, was one of the chines of Bournemouth which cut its way between high banks of gardens, villas and churches into the sea.

The days in July in which my possessions were delivered at the flat were sunlit and windless and everything I saw, the gay Dutch blinds, the patio, the tennis courts, the people whom my Victorian mother would have called 'nice' and my Victorian father 'gentlemanly' or 'decent', contrasted with the gross German bourgeoisie I had left, and as for the flat I had rented, my 'own' flat as it became in my mind, it had no great need of flowers to recommend its airy happiness.

Most of all it had become, instantly and intimately, a home. I had left behind the makeshift Mediterranean premises I had occupied, each of them having some gaping need, some irritating disadvantage, and found a home in England—not as I had dreamed of in Kent or Sussex in which I had been brought up, but in the far less familiar and genteel Bournemouth. I was home and dry, and confident of the future. There were new and old places waiting to be explored or re-examined, there were books waiting to be written and friends waiting to be discovered. There was the forest and the sea. There was enough space round my flat in which to grow as many plants as I wanted, and in Bournemouth shops (English shops in which I had not made purchases for the last twenty years) I could find food, wine and those things known only to householders which abroad must be searched for sometimes in vain, nail-clippers, face-flannels, tintacks or paperclips, cream cracker biscuits or thread (not cotton or silk) with which to sew on buttons securely, or angostura bitters. Only those who come home from long periods in exile know how much these apparently trivial etceteras 'mean to a tired heart'. So shops would be one of the 'advantages' of Bournemouth, as the forest and the sea, the Hardy associations and the family precedents were already.

Thus I slept my first night in that ground-floor flat of the absurdly-named Amira Court with the smell of garden flowers coming in through the French windows, with Joseph within earshot in the other bedroom, and woke to the realization that after so much journeying and experimenting in living I was home in a sea-coast English county. A tidy county full of villas and neat gardens, full of carefully dressed people, noisy with popular music, where the small English buns and cakes and loaves in normal shapes and sizes were displayed in the shops and sent out their familiar appetizing scent. The weather was endlessly discussed and politics were considered tedious and religion in bad taste.

I was not beginning an exciting life, as I had begun in so many surroundings in the past, but a comfortable rather uneventful one befitting my age and circumstances. A life conducive to writing which need not be unexciting, comfortable or uneventful, more than most of such writing. And with England, a vividly fresh country spread about me, with aspects unfamiliar and asking to be explored, there would be no lack of subject-matter. So I dressed to eat my first grateful breakfast in my new home.

Three

Bournemouth

That was enough, I decided, of house-hunting and talk about likely homes and rooms to be arranged. It was time to take all that for granted. I had enjoyed many kinds of zestful experiences in home-making in a large number of countries over many years and had written fondly trivial books about them, but now I intended—as a middle-aged Englishwoman in Tangier who was in love with a young man had put it—to *live*. She breathed the word, I remember, with vigorous emphasis to an audience of bar-loungers. Just how I would realize this aspiration I did not yet know, but I would find ways. The setting for such aims was right and I would accept it with gusto and content.

I began to look at Bournemouth, not in the light of family legends or of my own short memories, but as I realized it to be in fact. It is Victorian in the architecture of its churches, pubs, theatres and municipal buildings, Edwardian in street architecture and the layout of its parks, discreetly pluto-cratic in its residents, Midlands in its holiday-makers, swinging and cosmopolitan in its youth. Conifers and rhododendrons are prominent in its vegetation and chines in its topography. These made an interesting mixture, a town of character, a background for me of great variety. In spite of all the remains of the immediate past it is a youthful city, crowded with boys and girls of foreign nations who come here in the summer to learn English at one of the educational institutions. Its shopping areas are crowded by innumerable young working mums and factoryhand dads with their trailing children called to heel in broad

Brummagem voices. Perhaps most characteristic, I have to admit, are the respectable, rich older folk who are swallowed by the great villas set in highly cultivated gardens and who come out in their expensive clothes to use their credit accounts on one of the several large department stores round The Square, or to have 'mid-morning coffee' in the tea-rooms of 'the Stores', just as my Auntie Annie did at Philpots or Addison's in the pre-proletarian days of St Leonards-on-Sea.

A snobbish, stuffy town, you might say, where the shop assistants used such archaic terms as 'Sir' and 'Madam', and men wore regimental ties and heavy tweeds, and were in evidence with their wives at 'Eleven O'Clock Service' on Sunday morning. But you would, I think, be wrong in all but certain superficialities, and you would be missing the essential quality of the place which is 'old-fashioned' in the truest sense but 'modern' or 'with-it' in the minds, such as they are, of summer visitors. It is, in other words, an amalgam of styles and types, of periods and novelty, the whole primarily English but recognized as such most easily by those who have been brought up in similar surroundings. It has absolutely nothing in common with the towns from which I came to it, German or Mediterranean. I can recognize certain aspects of the Surrey of my boyhood but little of the more bluntly agricultural Kent or the Downland bareness of Sussex. I became quickly at home in it but eager to see and know more of its surroundings of woodland villages, unfamiliar place-names and the ubiquitous forest.

To this I addressed myself in the first months of taking up residence in Bournemouth, though I had to go out to Ringwood and from there make my way to Alan Blond's house. It was autumn now, the season which, especially in England, satisfies all my craving to see and scent the beauty of dying summer. It made me feel a countryman again and remember that all the out-of-school boyhood I had known was in Surrey, Sussex and Kent, which were rural when I knew them. I made no claim to be a naturalist or a student of wild life in any profound sense, though I knew it far better and more affectionately than I knew the cities I had lived in since those days. The New Forest was proverbially and until recently a camping place for gypsies, and I had been moving towards it by the route I had taken with my living-wagon and horse and ferret, and the *romani* Ted Scamp when we were crossing the southern counties. That the fall of France and my decision to join the Army had cut short that journey I still regretted, and I saw the New Forest partly as a glorious chance missed, and was determined to take advantage of this second opportunity.

A friend of Alan Blond's lent me a pony and trap, and I must use the hackneyed word 'thrill' for what I felt as I trotted silently over the soft ground between the trees, or saw the rusty bracken beside me. There were green and yellow leaves still hanging on the trees, though the beeches had lost their glorious colour. I saw furtive animals fleeing my path as I went, sometimes deer or smaller frightened creatures. I was intensely happy in the Forest, seeing into distances turning from grey to purple as the night came down. I had ridden over the hills in Morocco and along the beaches in Tunisia and Cyprus, but nothing I had experienced in those Mediterranean years filled me with quite the same mixture of ecstasy and nostalgia, the glorious sadness that comes with the dying year in England, when every creature, human and animal, is hurrying home before nightfall. And though I had never numbered the New Forest among delights I had promised myself, looking forward to England from abroad, it seemed that autumn to excel the beauty of all the landscapes in my years of exile. I could imagine nothing more rewarding than to trot along behind a pony, feeling that between the dripping trees there was a silence and intimacy I had not known since I walked through the woods in Kent. The wet rich smell of the leaves, the glimpses of animal and bird life, the absence in the autumn of vandals or chattering scatterers of litter and waste food, the sense of being in possession of the place— at least as much as anyone—and the gratitude I felt at being welcomed to a warm fire in Alan's big sitting-room and eating food that only the English want in the late afternoon, crumpets, cream, jam or home-made cakes. Above all, of being in England again after I had so long felt that I needed only the insistent sunlight of India or the Mediterranean.

I could not feel that the New Forest or Hampshire or Dorset were my homelands, as Kent and Sussex had been; they were areas of endless promise rather than of intimate recognition. One city within reach of Bournemouth I knew well, for in 1940 I joined that branch of the Army which was first called the Field Security Police, then when someone realized the mistake of confusing it with the Military Police became the Field Security Service and finally more pretentiously the Security Branch of the Intelligence Corps. When I chanced my future in joining this organization I was trained in an adopted theological college at Winchester. It had not been an altogether happy period, for I had soon realized my mistake in putting myself inescapably among a crowd of semi-cultured schoolmasters, claiming proficiency in some language and hoping that they would be used largely as interpreters or informants. How I eventually escaped by being commissioned in the Ghurkas and returning to Intelligence as a Field Security Officer, I have related in three of these books set in wartime, *The Licentious Soldiery*, *The Blood-Red Island* and *The Gorgeous East*, but in these I touched only lightly on my training in Winchester.

If my aim had been more introspective, I should have dwelt on it, for to me as to most civilian recruits in wartime, the first weeks of military discipline were fateful and I believe unforgettable. As usual I was an odd man out, since those around me had all lived under some sort of discipline —of work, of responsibility, of obligation, whereas I, as nearly as it was humanly possible, had enjoyed the freedom of a writer who could earn just enough money in his own time, by his own choice of occupation, to travel precariously and choose what companions he pleased. Admittedly I found after those first months of training and drill that by the exercise of the native cunning I found I possessed, I could evade nearly all restrictions, as any good Field

Security man, N.C.O. or officer should learn to do. But at Winchester for the first time since childhood I lived under regimentation; I became very consciously a disciplined soldier. Perhaps for that reason Winchester was vividly memorable to me, and now that I had come to live so near it I was resolved to make a visit to the city.

That was quickly possible, for my friend John Hitchcock, who had explored with me so many parts of the British Isles and continental Europe, came down with his wife and car at that time, and we set out for Winchester. Part of the training I had gone through was in motor-cycling, some beneficent brass-hat having decreed that a motor-cycle was essential to an F.S. N.C.O. I had owned one ten years before but now found that there had been primal changes in the thing so that acceleration was achieved by a twist of the wrist and gear changes by the feet. From the first I delighted in the sensation of having that power under me, the freedom and speed and exhilaration of the Matchless I had learned to ride. Afterwards I rode it through the length of England and through the snow in Scotland, accompanied it when it was carried ashore by naval ratings on the beaches of Madagascar, or scattered the red soil of that uncanny island, and afterwards 'not without dust and heat' in India, till I had regretfully left it behind me to be given a station-wagon when I was promoted to a Field Security officer. That autumn morning in 1973, motoring in John's car just thirty years after our landings in Madagascar, brought back not foreign travel but the despair of the A.A. scouts who had been conscripted and promoted to M.T. sergeants when my schoolmasterly comrades were learning to motor-cycle along the Hampshire roads. At a point approaching Winchester I recognized the slope on which we practised hill-climbing and one of those A.A. scouts, Sergeant Groves, helped me, a perspiring wretch, 'with the strange device—Excelsior' written all over me, to go upwards between rabbit-holes and ridges to the summit. The day of my return to Winchester had pale sunlight and dry leaves as I drove comfortably along, remembering my sweaty recruitment in the city ahead where today—I still found it difficult to realize—I should join with John and his wife in choosing a restaurant and looking round the buildings which had become now a teachers' training college. What curious and derisory tricks memory plays one!

We lunched at the Southgate, which has changed of course in the thirty years since I had played darts nightly there and dined with Eddie Bates in its excellent restaurant, and I remembered all the good fellows of the Rifle Brigade who had been my opponents on the board, and Julyan Pickering who was my 'oppo' (as I learned to call it when I was attached to the Royal Marines) in my own 'shower'.

For some reason I had rarely thought of my early years in the Army since I was released in 1946, but that day in Winchester brought it back to me, the autumn leaves falling on the road where we had marched and countermarched, the bellowing drill-sergeants and the relief of escaping to the Naafi to eat warm buns and drink not so warm coffee in the break. I saw the little house of the C.O. where his wife, a kindly soul who realized what it meant for me to sit in a comfortable chair by a drawing-room fire and drink hot tea and chatter freely about the depot, had invited me for an hour or two. She told me that her sister signed her letters to her as Judy O'Grady, and recognizing the allusion I laughed with her.

So with John and Marjorie I drove past the house and round King Alfred's College (commandeered as our depot) which seemed to have grown since that time. It was broad daylight as we went, but perhaps at night-time ghosts walked and sergeants' voices were heard faintly echoing on the breeze, or at least I imagined so as we turned to come again prosaically to Bournemouth. So I had achieved at least one of the visits I wanted to make again now that I lived in this region.

Why was that visit so important? Was it that I wanted to be sure that the recollections which had stuck obstinately in my mind while I had travelled such a long and varied road were accurately recalled still—or was it to feel the warmth of the few friends I had made and the fewer days of happiness I had passed outside the discipline and ugliness of the depot? My memories of these were far less sombre than I had imagined, for even there, even in an orderly depot among trainees for whom I had no respect or liking, I succeeded in finding radiant hours and touches of humour to be shared with others.

Thank God I had long since cured myself of the vice of keeping up with the Joneses or caring whether or not the house in which I lived was a place to be admired or even envied by people who came to visit me there. I had been touched by this vice in London before and after the war, at Ticehurst and in Tangier, though in the last-named the ambition was fading, and in the various places I had inhabited since then it had passed away. From Ireland, in a sudden burst of decision which I have never regretted, I had cases packed and despatched to Christies all of the watercolours, pottery, Oriental items, porcelain and books which I had collected through the years, and now in the furnished flat I occupied in Bournemouth I had only a few relics of my collecting days, some beautiful Indian bronzes, two paintings given me by their artists, Clifford Hall and Gui Harloff, a few good rugs, two or three carvings and other oddments, enough to give a personal touch to the rooms which had been furnished for someone else. In those first few months in Bournemouth I felt no pressing urge to decorate the interior of the house or the little patio on the south side, but old habits are hard to kill, and to compensate for the gaps left by coloured porcelain I purchased a collection of animals created by a local potter in reproduction of the animals found in the New Forest. They are beautifully made in brown, grey and cream with minutely observed naturalness—a Forest pony, a pair of squirrels, grey and red, a family of three foxes set in a convincingly natural group, an owl, a gerbil, a hare, an otter with her cub, a hedgehog, a badger and a frog. There was a long shelf over the valance and put on this they gave me as much pleasure, almost, as the majolica and faïence they had replaced.

41

Another old interest was given play now that I had settled in Bournemouth—the subject of my first book of culinary essays, *English Cooking*. In a modern catch-phrase 'I *like* it'. I can understand a man preferring *Tripe à la môde de Caen* to our blanched tripe and onions, though I must say I prefer the latter which seems to me more cleanly prepared and inviting; I can even forgive someone who thinks *Homard Thermidor* is better than cold boiled lobster; but what I can't take is the conversation in Anglo-French of so-called gourmets whose form of snobbery is to believe that every French dish is better than its English counterpart and that the French way of cooking game, for instance, comes anywhere near our own, and that any Continental dish, French, Italian or German, transcends our own ancient and magnificent steak and kidney pudding. I have boasted of my faith in certain English dishes before now in these books, and returning to an English town where most of our foods are obtainable, I name it as one of the rewards of having returned to live in England. I have had splendid dishes in many parts of the world and described them in print, and I do not want to belittle them now. But I do want to praise not only the dishes of Britain but the materials obtainable here, even when they come from supermarkets.

I shall be influenced in this by the strong force of nostalgia and the taste, common to most of us in later life, for the things to which we grew accustomed in childhood. I even admit that these may become idealized in memory. For instance, breakfast cereals. The two most common and most advertised in the first decades of the century were 'Force' and 'Grape-Nuts'. Were they really so much better than 'Weetabix' or 'Corn Flakes' of today? Or am I influenced by the fact that our family nurse used to cut out the familiar figures of 'Sunny Jim', which adorned packets of 'Force', and set them marching round the picture rail in the nursery? Is it because we used to be given a spoonful of sweetened condensed milk with our 'Grape-Nuts' to which that cereal adhered in a ball that makes me remember it so fondly? Who can tell? All the days of childhood either blazed with sunlight or covered the windowpanes with rime so that we were told that Jack Frost, a magical exciting caller, had visited us in the night. All we can say more prosaically is that we have a taste, generally speaking, for the food we liked in childhood, whether it is considered gastronomically laudable or not.

So I began to realize after all those years of wandering through picturesque and many-coloured markets abroad that many of the foods I had missed could now be obtained in plenty, though many exotic delicacies may be missing now. I had been offered in Cyprus, Tunis and Tangier a kind of salt fish which even when soaked for twenty-four hours bore no relation to the superb kipper or even better the Yarmouth bloater of home, while nothing in Scandinavia or Germany, countries where skill in smoking and salting fish is paramount, is comparable to our smoked cod's roe. As I write this I am relieved to hear that the Royal Navy has been sent into waters claimed by the plutocratic and piscatorial Icelanders who do nothing but tin their glutted sea-harvest. I know of no threat to our delicious whitebait or to the anchovies from which the firm of Burgess makes its anchovy paste, and both can be found in Bournemouth shops, while excellent shellfish can be purchased on the harbourside at neighbouring Poole. (I am told that most of it is brought from fishing grounds farther west, or even from Billingsgate, but in any case it is fresh and tempting.)

Smoked haddock can be found nearer my home and it is a relief to discover that owing to the so-called 'cod war' it is more frequently true smoked haddock rather than the long flat slabs of smoked cod which make only an inferior kedgeree, of which the name but not the nature of the dish comes from South India. Oysters, I believe, are being farmed off the Cornish coast but I trust none of them which are not natives of Whitstable or Colchester or, as I have learned to add after living in Ireland, the luscious oysters of Galway Bay. Lobsters and crabs are obtainable at not too inflated a price in Bournemouth and Poole, but more frequently one finds the coarse and rather tasteless crayfish whose claws are negligible and whose flesh is difficult to masticate.

I can remember buying herring at a ha'penny a piece in a city as distant from the sea as Cheltenham in the 1930s, and even though it is now weighed and sold at more than 50p a pound I still find it delectable when I can afford it. It was famous for having been cheap because it was so plentiful, but now it is both plentiful *and* expensive, which contradicts its reputation but does not make it less eatable.

Since I had been concerned with catering for myself and for Joseph, there have been, I find, significant changes apart from the arrival of supermarkets. Many shops have disappeared altogether, though their wares are sometimes offered by department stores, which never seems the same thing. Fish shops themselves are few, and where can be found a poulterer's with pheasants and partridges hanging above one's head, or hares, with their heads in a cup to catch the blood, or rabbits or guinea-fowl on hooks? More inexplicable, and annoyingly so in Bournemouth which is so near the New Forest, it is difficult if not impossible to find a joint of venison. But apart from these we can still count our blessings, even though we have to go to a supermarket to do so, and find many things unobtainable abroad. There are sausages of a kind; poor things, admittedly, compared with the sausage of the past, but still obtainable along with mass-manufactured pork pies, haggis, Cornish pasties and sausage rolls unrecognizable as those we once enjoyed. I suppose we must be thankful that something of a worthy tradition still exists.

Do you remember the excellence of a Bath Chap? Or pickled pork as a sideboard dish at breakfast? There are crumpets to be found in shops but never, as they were as late as the 1930s in London, brought round the quieter streets by a muffin-man with a handbell. Have you ever risen early and gone out in the dew-soaked fields to gather mushrooms? If so, you will know how infinitely superior they are to the artificially forced mushrooms sold at exorbitant prices today.

I learned from gypsies to ask for a 'knuckle end' in shops where they sliced their own bacon and offered you a choice of back or streaky till the last cuts were left on the bone and sold, I remember, for sixpence apiece. I find that I can still buy a 'knuckle end' at a few shops where I am favoured, but this gristly and almost meatless remnant today costs sixty new pence. Still, it is obtainable, as bacon is in various qualities, pink and white and distinguishably English, as opposed to the salty and leanless cooking fat sold as bacon abroad.

For how long shall we keep that descendant of the hero who once drove a rattling cart carrying a huge polished can, five foot tall, from door to door calling 'Milk-o' in friendly tones twice a day? He still arrives with the dawn and a reputation for befriending housewives, but I fear that he will soon be found uneconomical as the breadman and paper-boy have been found, or like Carter Paterson who once stopped wherever he saw a card in the window, or the coalman, woodman or deliveryman who has disappeared with 'modern times'. Yet while we still have a milkman who will also (if you can ever catch him) deliver cream, let us bless his name, for almost nowhere abroad does he come with any regularity or with anything but unreliable milk. It may be very romantic to have a herd of goats driven up and milked at your door, and I have no doubt that goats' milk is nutritious and dietetically desirable, but I am conventional enough to prefer a pinta delivered in a hygienic bottle at my door out of reach of the blue-tits who have learned to pierce the foil over it.

Fruit and vegetables can still be bought according to the season, and although there is all the difference in the world between garden-grown and field-grown products, we can *in theory* grow our own strawberries, peas, raspberries, gooseberries and asparagus, and these, the fruits and vegetables which most repay care and garden soil, are better in our own country than abroad.

It was from my father that I learnt—not to cook, for he was the most unhandy man, and I'm glad that he died before the sinister phrase 'do-it-yourself' became current—but to shop, wisely, variously and pleasurably. After leaving 'the House', as the Stock Exchange was invariably called by its members, he would go to Leadenhall Market to buy a joint for his family, and I would frequently accompany him. He was known to the stall-keepers and no buyer for a large restaurant was treated with more appreciation. 'What about that little piece over there?' he would say, and the butcher would use his long pole with a hook on it to reach it down for him. But even at this late date I remembered with gratitude my father's skill in purchasing, for I had inherited a little of its prudence and rewards. I knew of many foods scarcely known outside England, plebeian many of them but none the worse for that, and I learned that they could still be found in Bournemouth. I knew also how to treat them in the traditional way—how to make a Melton Mowbray pork pie, a Lancashire hotpot or Cornish pasties which made the products of mass catering and manufacture look dull and be, in my father's words, a 'wicked waste of money'.

I suppose it would be considered a vulgar habit on a seaside holiday to buy a pint of shrimps and bring them home to be devoured with bread and butter and tea, but I rejoiced in it when shrimps were sold by the pint by the men who pushed monster nets through the surf to catch them; I suppose it would be unspeakable to buy winkles and eat them with a pin but I would do it today if winkles were any longer sold in the street.

I wonder if any head of a household has the remains of a sirloin grilled to make a breakfast dish for himself, as my father did, or 'brings down from London' to his Home Counties home a heap of scallops which could be prepared and served to his family on the same evening, or purchases marrow-bones from which their delicate contents will be extracted for a 'savoury'? It would be as well if more housewives today knew how to souse mackerel or regard as a luxury beef dripping with natural aspic an inch thick to be eaten on hot toast.

At Christmas time an enormous York ham would be sent

to my father by some grateful client ('I made a lot of money for that man') and from another a complete Stilton cheese as big as a drum, from which we dug portions with a cheese scoop for weeks afterwards. Some parodies of all these things are obtainable today and in Dingles' Food Store, our most enterprising shop, we can still sometimes find them. I am grateful for this and am glad I have come to live in England where *familiar* food, rather than the exotic and luxurious delicacies of the Mediterranean, is sold at not too ruinous a price. Yes, I sometimes miss mangoes, calamares, the plentiful truffles of North Africa and other delights I have known for twenty years, but I am willing to forfeit them all for the old gastronomic friends I have found here.

Four
Smarden and Chipstead

One of the happiest realizations to me in having returned to England was that I could be driven, in action and reality, to places which existed more visibly in my memory than on the map. As I had done, for instance, to Winchester to re-live my months as a recruit, and as I resolved to do now to Smarden, that Wealden village in which my father had died, in which I had afterwards lived in his home.

Smarden, in fact, was alive with vistas and characters of the past and scenes which haunted me, though it was twenty years since I had set eyes on them and thirty since they had been the everyday background of my life. I remembered clearly the group in the churchyard when my father was buried and his brother, whom he invariably called 'that scoundrel', appeared unexpectedly for the funeral, so that I met him for the first time since childhood, and two of my mother's brothers, my uncles Edward and Stanley ('Toby') Taylor, having come to support my mother who had scarcely left my father's side for forty years and was to live another thirty without him. I remembered, too, the plans I had made when I had come to live in Smarden Grange, my father's last house of all the 'beautiful little places' he had enthusiastically described to my poor mother and which he left after a year or two when some other home had attracted him. Smarden Grange was a very early Victorian house with rooms too large for me and an orchard planted with Conference pears, and a greenhouse in which I grew tomatoes.

Finally I remembered the last Smarden episode when I

had bought for £10 a magnificent gypsy living-wagon and a sturdy carthorse. The wagon stood in an orchard owned by three old brothers, Harry, Libby and Edgar Homewood, the last Kentish yeomen who truly deserved the name whom I was to know in my life. I have described them elsewhere—Harry, stumping along on his short legs like one of the Seven Dwarfs and with a devotion to fish and game, birds and beasts of the countryside which (though not in literacy or articulateness) could be rivalled only by Jack Hargreaves; Edgar, who was the man of the world of the three, having left Smarden for two years in the trenches in World War One; and Libby, who had lost a leg in that war and was the cook and general housekeeper for the others. I had watched Harry shoot a fox crossing a snow-covered field at a hundred yards' distance, and Harry and Libby bringing out their baskets of stored apples to be turned into cider by the itinerant owner of an old cider press. I had eaten the game they gave me, rabbits, a hare or a partridge, while I lived in the gypsy wagon waiting for the snow to melt so that I could set out on my journey. I knew now that the last of the three, Edgar, had died twenty years ago but I wanted to see Smarden again, and while I was staying with John and Marjorie Hitchcock in Underriver, which was not too far distant, I asked John to drive me over.

The wife of a retired Admiral who now lived in Smarden had asked me for a photograph to illustrate a manuscript history of the village and its residents which she was compounding, and I called on her and her husband and sister before I examined the churchyard in which my father had been buried. It was just as well I did so, for afterwards I was too angry to speak and have remained angry, if not speechless, ever since. My mother, with sentiments which will be understood by all her contemporaries and by many of her juniors, had caused to be erected an inscribed head-stone over my father's grave. I knew exactly where he had been buried and went to the place, only to find that the headstone had been removed. Until her death my mother had posted a quarterly sum to the sexton, but I gathered he had died not long before my visit and no one could tell me anything about the missing stone.

I suppose I must admit to having been more an anti-Anglican than a good Catholic, and this roused all the enmity which I had once felt towards parsons. I remembered the curate who had tried to seduce me as a boy of fourteen and all the other clergymen against whom I had felt unreasoning resentment. I searched the churchyard and saw other headstones which had been removed from their places and piled against a wall, but my father's was not amongst them.

No one could explain or even suggest an explanation. The worst of it was that my father, though admittedly not the most devout of churchmen, had expressed a wish to my mother during his last illness that he should be buried in that churchyard, feeling that after all the moves from home to home he had made in his life, in Smarden he had eventually come to rest.

I did everything I could to find the truth. The Rector, a recently appointed man named Canon Phillips, also made enquiries, and after I wrote to the Registrar of the Diocese of Canterbury, I received the following letter:

'I am in receipt of your letter of the 4th June, addressed to the Commissary General of the Diocese of Canterbury, and I am very sorry to hear the headstone on your late father's grave has been removed.

'A faculty was issued on the 20th December 1954 authorizing the levelling of mounds over graves in Smarden Churchyard, the lifting up of certain footstones and the placing of these against the appropriate headstones, and on the 28th July 1966 a further faculty was issued authorizing the removal of kerbstones around untended graves. No other work was authorized by these faculties. I do not know what can have happened to the headstone on your father's grave and in view of the enquiries made by Canon Phillips it would seem there is now no person in the parish who can throw any light on the matter.

'In the circumstances I am afraid I must say that after this lapse of time there are no steps which can be taken by the Ecclesiastical Authorities and I can only say I am sorry the headstone should have completely disappeared.'

So there, apparently, it must rest. I am the sole surviving son of my father and feel with distress and anger that his body was entrusted to the care of the Church of England, and employees or members of that Church have betrayed the trust. Perhaps it would have been better if I had not felt the reasonable and not at all morbid impulse to visit his grave. There is no one to join me in my indignation, for my sister prefers not to recall the incident. What my Victorian mother with the ardent Protestantism which had made her resent my becoming a Catholic would have said, I hate to imagine. At least let me appeal to any reader of this book who may have read all this with interest. Should a man expect to rest quietly in his grave in a Christian churchyard for a century or two, or should he not? Barring, of course, hostile bombs or earthquakes? I furiously maintain that he should and curse the Anglican officialdom which had accepted the fees for burial and a place in the churchyard, then caused his headstone if not his remains to be removed from the place he chose.

But I made another return to the past that autumn which was far happier and more rewarding. I went back not by a year or two to a period just before the Second World War but to another age, no less vivid to me, revisiting that village on the Surrey Downs in which we had lived from 1907 to 1914. It was this little Green Belt village of Chipstead that I described in *The Gardens of Camelot* and again, less faithfully, in my novel *Under the Rose Garden*.

Returning to it on a bright day in early spring, just sixty years after I had left it, was a very curious experience in double vision and double experience, for if I was unrecognizable even to myself as the little boy who walked beside Ninna, or later beside my sister and Miss Wain, I *felt* very much as I did then, surprised to find discreet new houses standing back from the village street where no houses, as I very well remembered, had been. But a landmark, the village shop, was still there, although its wares were displayed like those of a miniature supermarket. I resist the folksy suggestion that I expected to see the Philips brothers, or the Philipses as they were called, waiting behind the counter to weigh a few ounces of bullseyes or currant biscuits, but it is a fact that after I left the shop a middle-aged woman breathlessly caught me up in the street and said she was the grand-daughter or great-niece of one of 'the Philipses'—the one with the bright red cheeks and a beard—and remembered as I did how the inmates of Cane Hill Asylum, wearing their grey workhouse uniforms, had walked in a crocodile once a week to the shop to buy the few penceworth of sweets allowed them in those harsh Dickensian days, while old Mr Tucker, a rich lunatic, who had a keeper to accompany him everywhere from his comfortable house, moved with freedom about the village.

It is in details of this kind that a memory like mine becomes sometimes painful. My childhood was a happy and plentiful one but the meaning of historical events, unlike domestic details, was entirely lost to me. My father, a prosperous stockbroker at that time, was considered to overpay his gardener at 30/- a week and kept two domestic servants and a nurse for the children, while I remember the 'loyal railwaymen' on the London–Brighton line subscribing to present him with an umbrella for the good work he had done in raising a large subscription among the commuters (who were called season-ticket holders in those days) to reward them for staying at work during a strike. I remember wearing a purple rosette, as every other Tory child wore, for the General Election, and the ferocious abuse of Lloyd George which makes present day abuse of Tony Benn sound mild in comparison. I can remember the village pump from which many of the cottages drew water to be carried to their tiny rooms, made even more stuffy and more crowded by the geraniums in their poky windows, and I remember barefoot children whose parents had been unable to keep up their subscriptions to the thrift boot club organized at the time. No wonder the Surrey Downs on which we picnicked were beautifully unpopulated—who had leisure to enjoy them but the few tenants of comfortable houses for the middle-class families who were immigrants in the village? Such things never clouded my childhood, how indeed could they? And they only cloud the memory of that time now in my more mature perceptions.

That day in the early months of 1974 gave me, in the schizophrenic ways I have described, some intensely happy hours. I met in The White Hart, which I entered for the first time, an elderly man who had been a youngster when I lived in Chipstead and was what I believe is called a mine of information. No one living in the village today was there when I was young. An architect named Scott-Willey whom I described in *The Gardens of Camelot* was the last to die. All the rest of those I remembered had gone long since, the Rector, Prebendary Stone, a *Punch* artist, Talbot Smith, with his tall kind wife, Sir Horace Marshall, a wholesale stationer who later became Lord Mayor of London in Armistice Year—which my father considered almost a desecration, the Goads, the Trittons, the Freemans with their tall daughter Winifred, the distinguished Colonel Cochran who lived at Purbright, Dr Tudge and Dr Rowe, the lay reader with the enlarged Adam's apple, Mr Adams, Mrs Thyer, our bad-tempered but brilliant cook, the Fulshams, the farm kept by Mrs Flint, and another where an Old Tonbridgian Captain Lenham was the first village casualty in 1914, the Ashdowns, Dr Freshfield known as a traveller and a Freeman of the City of London, the Strakers, the Bulls, the Campbell-Coopers and the Lamberts. Not only had they all gone but they had left no descendants behind them, so that Chipstead knew nothing of them or their memories.

More dramatically I heard news of that beloved hero of my childhood, our 'knife-and-boot' boy Leslie Beadle. In *The Gardens of Camelot* I wrote of him and of my rebellious determination to make him my friend.

'It was conceded by authority that Beadle was a very nice knife-and-boot boy, the most industrious and the best-mannered we had ever had. He looked, in fact, almost angelic when he sang in the choir on Sundays, with his fair hair and blue eyes and clean surplice. There was nothing against Beadle, but it was "not the proper thing", it was "not right", it "would never do" for me to go about with him. He might use "rough language"; I might pick up curious information. In any case, what would people say?

'I knew by some half-formed instinct that he was a fine boy, honourable, humorous, gay. He was older than I by about four years, old enough to join up two years later and be killed on the Somme. He was generous and patient with a little boy's questions. So, unaware that I was showing the form of all my future life, unaware of any significance at all in what I did, I defied the ban imposed.

'After all, how could my parents understand my frantic excitement in knowing that tomorrow Beadle was bringing his ferret to work so that I could examine this fabulous creature so often described in sagas of downland rabbiting? Or of my hearing, on Monday morning, the events of Beadle's one free day? Or of using his catapult? All these would have seemed to them unimportant compared with the impropriety of the friendship. So it remained clandestine and had the added fillip of all secret and illicit things.'

'Killed on the Somme', you will notice, and so I had long understood the fact to be. But the cousin to Leslie Beadle, a retired chauffeur in his sixties, came into The White Hart that morning and told me what I should have been thrilled to hear a few decades earlier that our 'knife-and-boot boy', though he had indeed joined the Army and fought on the Somme, had not been killed but had lived in fact until a year or two ago. Oh well—it may be as well that I did not learn of this till after he was dead. He could scarcely have been expected to live up to the idealized portrait I had built of him in my mind. The most I might have found if I had returned to Chipstead earlier was a good darts-player with whom I might have 'taken on the best two in the house' instead of the wonderboy friend of my childhood.

I suppose that among Arcadian memories I must pay the penalties by retaining a number of vindictive and vengeful ones no less clear and real than those. A psychologist would make mincemeat of me on the strength of them, proving that I was absurdly sensitive, vain and querulous as a child. I daresay I was, but I am not so now, more than half a century later, and for years I could still reawaken resentment at the snubs I received from my elders, who can never have foreseen this unforgiving memory of mine.

My dear mother's sins of this kind came later but even then they were painful. On a half-term exeat from my preparatory school I joined my mother and some adult ladies in the summer-house, and the thrill of a holiday having gone to my head perhaps, I asked at tea for a second helping of strawberries and cream. My mother told me kindly that I should have realized there were not many for everyone, and I fled with fiery cheeks to a refuge farther down the garden. It was my poor mother also—never my father—who would send me out of earshot of her conversations with grown-ups. But it was my second brother Hubert (Bertie) who not only snubbed but bullied me all through our childhood, so that I detest his memory almost to this day. I realize now that he was a brainless, good-looking oaf, excessively selfish and crude, who seduced me without love and used his five years' seniority to treat me as an annoying child to be reduced to silence and tears whenever it was possible. Scarcely less brutal did the four brothers of my mother seem when I was young, though I have of course realized that they meant no cruelty. I can still hear my Uncle Edward, who lived near us in Woldingham, threatening me for not being good to my mother, Herbert the R.A.M.C. Colonel who never spoke to children, though his wife, my Auntie Emma, did what she called 'teasing' them perpetually. The third brother, my Uncle Horace, the

Chief Electrician of Swansea, who committed suicide later, considered me ungrateful and too talkative and showed it tartly, while only my Uncle Stanley ('Toby') Taylor was a hero to me in childhood and little more than a name afterwards. It was the fashion in those Edwardian days to 'sit on' 'uppish' children, and I daresay it did no harm. I can only say, as I demonstrate here, that I have remembered every snub from the age of seven to that of seventy and warn people in contact with children that one of them may have a memory as long as mine or as Burns said: 'A child's among you taking notes, And, faith, he'll print it.'

If all the good people I remembered in Chipstead had gone their way underground long before I visited the place in 1974, yet the village itself had changed surprisingly little. The pond, on which in winter we had skated and in summer had tried to reach the outspreading branches over the water on which was a moorhen's nest, was still unaccountably there, and cattle and horses, I was told, still drank at it. The little brick edifice of the village pump, perhaps from snobbishness or shame, had been pulled down, and the village forge which we had visited for repairs to be made to our go-cart was no more, though its site was occupied by a service station. 'Mr Barnard's' the ironmonger's had gone too, and it must have been many years since Mr Peckham advertised 'Teas 6d.' outside his cottage. But the church, in which suffragettes in 1913 had exploded a small bomb, still smelt of mustiness and sanctity, and although Shabden, the large mock-Gothic house, had become some kind of home, school or residential centre, the imitation moat which was part of its phony-antique attraction was still half full of fallen leaves, so that perhaps children kick their way through them as my sister and I did in the year of King George V's Coronation, the year in which I was sent to boarding school.

Skelton's Lane which we named after the Misses Skelton who lived in it had, I think, disappeared and our own home, Wayside, a large plaster-cast house which had been hidden behind shrubs at the end of the village road in my father's time, now stood shamelessly exposed and its name altered to something else. Beside it, covering the area which had been my father's proud half-acre of rose-trees, a new house had been built by one of the owners of Wayside after we had left the district.

Mr Cheeseman's big square white-painted Regency house had been bought after his death during World War One by another family. I learned of this from the cousin of Leslie Beadle who had been employed by them as a chauffeur for forty years and had now retired to their Lodge, from which he came to gossip with me in The White Hart. That he should have grown up, been employed for four decades and retired, all since the days I remembered so well seemed rather eerie to me, but I was grateful to him for all the information he gave me of dyings and departures, of the casualties of two wars, the enrichments and impoverishments of so many human beings I remembered, and for these alone I felt I had not returned to England in vain. Chipstead was not an ancient village fossilized among progressive neighbours; it was more fascinating than that, a dormitory district now as then, a district in which the only remarkable changes were those in its inhabitants. These demonstrated that the difference between the middle-class and the working-class, so pronounced then, had become scarcely visible to the eye or audible in the accents of either. Mr Barnard, who was called by my father a 'good-as-you-are' kind of fellow, would have merited not this reputation but its reality in fact if he had lived in Chipstead today, and the Goads and the Trittons would no longer be acknowledged as the aristocracy of the village. I liked to think that in my own way I had done more to bring this about than the intellectual Socialists I knew, even if it was through the medium of darts and beer, and minor personal rebellion against my own class. It should never be forgotten of homosexuals or men of homosexual mind that whatever their motives, they are the best levellers, the least class-conscious of all the minorities in the world, and that this has created the enmities from which they suffer. They can be forgiven for taking a lover of their own social status but observers are always critical of an intellectual or aristocratic man who loves—as many of them do—a handsome but illiterate peasant. In my own case the only corroborative evidence (necessary in a case of this kind) which the prosecuting conspiracy by which I was attacked could bring was the fact that the witnesses were uneducated sailors. Why else, the high-minded prosecutors asked, would a man educated at a public school and acknowledged as a reputable writer, why else would such a man invite to his home a couple of simple matelots? But that was all more than twenty years ago when I sat sharing pints in The White Hart with Leslie Beadle's cousin and another worker, or munched sandwiches with the barman in the 'public' in an inn that was scarcely mentionable in my family when I had last been in Chipstead before the outbreak of World War One.

Towards Christmas of that year the past was recalled to me vehemently by the sight of a poster advertising a circus programme in which Derrick Rosaire was to appear. It brought back instant memories of those summer days before the war when I had bought a trailer caravan and gone tenting with the Rosaire family circus, first across the Yorkshire Moors and south to Lincolnshire, when I had written the story of their family in *The Circus Has No Home*, and in the following year across the Southern counties till we were halted by the outbreak of war. I wrote then that I was not deeply attracted to any one of them but was in love with the whole family, and as nearly as such words can be, it was true. So in that Christmas time of 1974 I immediately telephoned the theatre where Derrick Rosaire would be appearing and arranged to come and see him.

Nothing could so forcefully demonstrate the years that had passed as his appearance. He was a young man of thirty-odd, not the Derrick I expected, the youngest of the eight Rosaire sons and daughters, but the son of Ivor, the other brother who had toured Europe with me in a living-wagon. This Derrick had been named after this uncle who was now nearing sixty years old and had been in America with his wife and grown-up children for years. Derrick Junior brought his wife, daughter of another circus family, and infant Hercules of a son to my home, and I learnt that the Countess had died only a year or two ago, outliving as she was determined to do Madame Paulo, that other circus matriarch; that Dennis spent most of his time in Spain, as he might be expected to do from his Hispanophil nature and Spanish marriage; that Ida's son had inherited her dog-act and that Cissie and Vivienne were queens of the fair-ground world into which they had both married.

They stayed for a long time giving me all the news of the family and the circus which had once been so familiar to me, when I wrote of each occasion that I had been with any of the family, who had numbered ten at that time. Even now I would have set out in any kind of vehicle to follow them through the counties if their circus had not long since folded its tents for the last time and left its performers scattered about the world. That conversation with a man and his wife I had never met was the most truly nostalgic in my experience.

Five

A Stroke

On Good Friday, 12th April, 1974 (this precision is because for the first time in my life I purchased and tried to make entries in a desk diary), I was sitting with Joseph watching television when I was called to the next room to answer the telephone and found that my right leg had become unreliable. At first I thought it had 'gone to sleep' but when I returned to my armchair I realized that it was partially paralysed.

These personal details are, I hope, uncharacteristic of this series of books in which I have shown myself occupied with the world and the people about me, and have not dwelt on egocentric details which appear to occupy most autobiographers who are more interesting to mankind than I am, by reason of their reputation or achievements. My excuse for dealing with the stroke (as it turned out to be) which partially crippled me from that evening onwards, is that some such arterial affliction happens to the majority of Western people at some time between growth and death, so that I am writing of a common misfortune, giving a personal interpretation to nearly universal incidents.

At first I dismissed it as some momentary mischance caused perhaps by my habit of crossing one leg over the other for long periods, but before I went to bed I realized that I could not walk unaided or raise my right leg or arm. Joseph, as usual, remained admirably calm, helped me to bed and telephoned our National Health doctor, who was one of a group of practitioners. He was away for Easter but one of his colleagues came next morning.

'You've had a little stroke,' he said cheerfully, and I began to calculate the probable effects.

Our own doctor came on Tuesday, and raised the question of my going into hospital but was checked by Joseph who said he could and would look after me in our home. This was a far bigger undertaking than it appeared, since I was now quite unable to move my right arm or leg, and the task of nursing me was onerous and demanding. The doctor could do little for me but make cheering visits and prescribe, while I procured the help of a physiotherapist. The most alarming aspect of it to me was that my right hand was quite useless, and as I have always written by hand everything from whole books to personal letters, I could not see the future with any confidence.

As I have repeatedly claimed, I despise the vice of self-pity in myself or others, but for a time it was hard to avoid some element of it. Like many men and particularly many bachelors, I have gone through my later years wholly unconscious of the threat of death by—to speak colloquially—not thinking about it. Illness till then had been a nuisance, an interruption in the pleasant continuance of my life and I had never had a bad accident. But this sense of being 'struck down', and not knowing what the consequences might be, left me numb and dismayed.

I mean no offence to feminists or even to the upholders of Women's Liberation when I say that I thanked God in those weeks that I had chosen a man as my lifelong companion, and one of such selfless devotion and understanding as Joseph. It will take a skilled nurse and a good psychologist to know what he went through then, with a man in his seventieth year, weighing fourteen stone, and worried about himself and doubting whether he would ever be able to make a living again. Joseph himself was nearing fifty now and, of course, occupied with his own affairs, his family and other emotional ties, but with his Indian sense of loyalty and fixity of purpose he brought us both through the crisis which followed.

Other help was coming. I have more than once remarked

in the course of these books, with more or less seriousness, that as one born under the sign of Gemini, I am prone to calamities, but that each misfortune as it comes will never be the worst that could happen. So it was now, though for a long time I could not foresee that. Within a week or two after Joseph had telephoned to my most intimate friends and relations, they began to arrive, and with each visit I grew more hopeful. First, as it happened, because it had been arranged some time before, a visit from Darrell and Susan Bates from their Cornish home. I had not seen them since staying with them in Gibraltar where Darrell had been Permanent Secretary. They came not knowing what to expect, for as I found out later, a stroke suggested to most people mental damage, speech difficulty and complete paralysis. The first realization that here again it had not been by any means 'the worst that could happen' gave me renewed confidence, and my sanguine nature began to assert itself. Darrell and Susan were cheering, too, and Darrell and I talked literary shop for an hour before they had to return to Land's End.

Then my brother Geoffrey, the youngest and most 'reliable one of the family', whose wedding I described in *The Sound of Revelry*, motored down as soon as he had heard of my mishap, as he had raced to every sick-bed and death-bed in the family for years, and to everyone who needed his advice and assistance. He had suffered as I had from having to compete with the charisma (for once the word is correctly used) of our dear, weak, popular but volatile brother, Laurie. Geoffrey had 'made his own life', as each of us had done, and fathered two now grown-up sons, one of whom is my godson Derek. Geoff, when he came to Bournemouth, was at once practical and set about finding the necessary means to bring the television set through from the sitting-room, so that it faced my bed at a sufficient distance and gave me something to occupy—if not perhaps my mind—at least my eyes and attention. This in itself made me very grateful, but what perhaps did more was the realization he brought me that I was not alone in the family sense, that at least one of my few living relatives responded to Joseph's call. It was, then, a most stunning blow when two months after he had come down to see me, my brother Geoff died suddenly of totally unsuspected cancer of the kidneys.

Soon after Geoff's visit to Bournemouth came my cousin Stephen Oliver, my uncle Edward Taylor's grandson, who less than a year before had come to my seventieth birthday party in Monschau in the Rhineland. A barrister, who used to turn up in Tangier with undergraduate friends while he was up at Oxford, he had become a family man with a charming wife named Dawn and three children. But he found time to come down and, practical as Geoff, immediately went out to buy me a bedside table which proved its essential value within an hour of my receiving it.

Then, of course, John Hitchcock, my lifelong friend, left the Board of which he is Chairman to find the Bournemouth flat, and his son, my second godson, who is a don at Exeter University, drove up and assisted Joseph to deal with my literary affairs. Donald Ebrahim, my friend and Joseph's, came from his busy medical practice in Coventry and added professional advice to the practical and personal kind that I was receiving.

I felt myself an immensely lucky man. I had always regarded friendship as the first consideration in my motley life and had been blessed with friends of many callings, nationalities, characters and classes. On many occasions in my life I have been grateful to them, but never more than in those weeks of spring 1974.

So from the black depression of my first days of illness my gusto started to assert itself and I began, as by nature I am bound to do, to see the brighter aspects of what had been insoluble problems, and so to count my blessings. The first of these was Joseph and it is impossible to exaggerate the care he gave me or the gruesome duties of nursing a man who cannot move. Then I had a comfortable little home, warm and friendly if not spacious or stately. Lying in bed I would soon be able to see from my windows young people playing tennis and hear their cheery calling across the court;

I could see, too, the squirrels running up to the bird table and carrying away the peanuts put out for them, and the birds, who were unafraid of them, pecking their seed under the squirrels' sharp little noses.

The telephone was beside me, *The Times* came regularly, and Joseph cooked the food I liked and gave me the whisky and water that I was allowed. Within two months I could hobble through to the bathroom with the aid of a stick, and though I could not yet shape my handwriting, I believed that within a year or so I should be able to do so, well enough at least to form recognizable hieroglyphics with which I should be able to make my meaning intelligible.

Although in fact there was a third stage of my affliction coming to me, I had no knowledge of it then, a stage in which I should realize that I was not going to recover any of my agility, that the walking and riding which I had always loved were lost to me, that I was to be at least half a cripple, in a word, for as long as I should live. Though even then I could be thankful that my brain was unaffected and that after a fashion I might be able to write again, I should cease to be the active man I had rejoiced in being. I would be driven back to the use of a car or some other vehicle, and that only if I could afford it. I should be given the sympathy, if not pity, which would condescendingly be shown to me, inevitably a matter of indignation, even anger, to one of my temperament. All that was to come when I should realize that the 'stroke' had left me with a permanently disabled leg and had for the remainder of my life forced me to adopt slower movements, thoughts, instincts and pleasures. In the meantime, in this second period, I was spoilt, lazy and content.

More so when I received an invitation from the *Spectator* to write *A Spectator's Notebook* for four weeks. The *Spectator* was a periodical to which I had first contributed half a century earlier (though doubtless the editor was unaware of that). *A Spectator's Notebook* has been written by a long list of distinguished contributors, including in fairly recent years Harold Nicholson and, after his death, for a time by Compton Mackenzie. It is intended to give the utmost freedom to anyone writing it to talk of anything he likes in whatever form, and it will be understood that having spent so much time staring at the Box, I chose Television as one of my subjects, making a number of personal enemies who seem to arise whenever I express opinions in print, justifiably no doubt.

I dictated the article, recalling that during the long but painless and not depressing months I had spent recovering in my own home, I had been disinclined for much reading or conversation and had been almost entirely dependent for time-passing and entertainment on a colour television set which stood facing my bed at a comfortable distance. From it I learned a great deal not only of television itself but the state of mind of people who become reputedly obsessed by it and watch it at all hours of the day and late into the night, who subordinate their social life and obligations to its demands. I have been made to realize how the thing has changed habits of thought and expression during the decade or two in which it has become (whether we like it or not) a dominant aspect of national life.

First I stress *colour* television, for whether or not the colours are natural or accurately reproduced on the screen, there is no doubt that they bring an element of reality to the changing picture, as anyone who has watched it and returns to black and white must be aware. Readers of news bulletins and weathermen whom we are accustomed to see looking ruddy and well-fed seem suddenly gaunt and liverish as though the colour had literally been drained from their cheeks, and the world becomes a lifeless place beyond the Styx.

I have watched television for long periods with understanding and interest in a number of countries, including our only European rivals in its production, France and Germany, and I am wholly convinced that our own, with its unique system of alternative national and commercial programmes, is now (so far as that goes) the best that the world has to give.

I must however say, voicing of course only one individual's prejudices, that perhaps inevitably and through the failures of our nature and our national economy at least seventy per cent of programmes created for television are mediocre and unimaginative and that the rest, sport, news of topical events, political propaganda and the reproduction of old films, are gravely deficient from the standpoint of the viewer, though he is nearly always willing and ready to be pleased and entertained. Programmes of political propaganda must of necessity be shown at the same time on all channels, or we should be able by manipulation to escape listening to their banalities, but why should the same system of coercion be applied to sporting events and, far more exasperating, to the exchange of boring views and comments by the 'experts' who are employed to discuss them? One appreciates the necessity of filling time by the showing of old films retired from service in the cinema long since, but why do these always seem to be chosen for the sake of the maximum boredom by the greatest number of viewers of mixed and contrasting interests?

We are anxious for the news to be read twice and sometimes three times during the evening, and appreciate that it is accurately and intelligently read by skilled newscasters, but why should the by-products of news, trivia and personalities, opinion and would-be amusing experiences of reporters occupy so much time after the news proper? Surely the reminiscences of nonagenarians, the old-time skills of artisans, the appearance in the provinces of actors or the tricks and perfections of favourite pets, all described to inquisitive interviewers, do not merit quite so much of the time of tired workers coming home and expecting to be entertained by their favourite programmes?

Among these the highest talent, creative, inventive or merely interpretative, seems to be that of individual or twin comics who have more of it than all the versatile actors, the wily interviewers, the quizmasters, debaters, descriptive artists and musicians put together. In their acts, it seems to me, lives the only true and individual genius to be seen on

66

television. There are doubtless able playwrights, both serious and sprightly, and a quite uncannily large number of talented actors and actresses able to extract the last spark of significance from their scripts, but I only feel myself in the televised presence of an immortal when one of these rare spirits appears and takes me to another, infinitely funnier and larger, world.

I am thinking, of course, of Morecambe and Wise, with their apparent spontaneity which conceals, I suspect, stern dedication; of the Two Ronnies of whom the debate eternally continues, which is the funnier? Joyce Grenfell, the only true comic among women, the others being beautifully funny comediennes and actresses and in another category. Michael Crawford who has the divine gift of self-ridicule as well as that touch of pathos which only the greatest funny men seem to display; Stanley Baxter who possesses and enthrals his audience; and Mike Yarwood who reduces them to near-hysteria at the (usually willing) expense of his victims; Dick Emery who is a satirist as well as a comic; and Benny Hill who can be funny for a full hour without a single lapse into seriousness. The Goodies who so cleverly exploit the unexpected, and Tommy Cooper, Dave Allen and Frankie Howerd who in entirely different ways make me retch with laughter, and finally the lugubrious Les Dawson whose concealed affability makes his disgruntled manner wholly irresistible.

Comic situations in series, weekly episodes on a single theme or set in a similar background, have proved to be so successful initially that they have been too often and too long repeated. *Dad's Army* surprised everyone by its immense appeal and viewability, and I for one hope it continues for another year or two, as I hope for *It Aint't Half Hot, Mum* which has for me a nostalgic reality, truth of detail and verisimilitude I find almost sublimely funny. The same may be said of *Are You Being Served?* So also did I for a long time find *Till Death Us Do Part*, *Steptoe and Son* and *Father, Dear Father*, but others have been based on situations not strong enough to sustain a whole series of half-hour comedies and have died unregretted before to the general public their end was in sight.

The list of these is long, for it seems that only by releasing a number of episodes in such a series can the producers discover what the response to it will be, and most of those which have endeared themselves to the public have seemed at first of dubious appeal, or based on a situation which might arouse actual hostility or social self-consciousness like *Upstairs, Downstairs* or even *The Forsyte Saga*.

Frankly I want television to entertain rather than to educate me, so I keep my knobs unpressed for most programmes of archaeological, historical, or scientific interest. I make an exception for the gorgeous and informative details of old civilizations which Julius Norwich so articulately gives us, but I am not so receptive to Lord Clark, and thoroughly dislike the manner and matter of James Burke. The promoters (like Michael Parkinson, Russell Harty and David Frost) of intimate interviews with film stars and other already over-exposed personalities seem for the most part to be indulging in exercises in egomania, in spite of the near-hysterical appreciation of invited audiences.

Many of these strictures came from individual fads and disapprovals, but most habitual viewers could formulate similar lists. In this lies the strength and the weakness of the medium—strength because the promoters have to range far to find new kinds of programme, and weakness because believing they have found them, they work them to death.

For the rest, omitting public events, crowd scenes, royal occasions, discussions of topical issues, glimpses of wild life and exotic animals, which are nearly always rewarding, colourful scenes of travel, people of little-known races, of wars and disasters and violence, I remember as we all do when we meet in trains and at meals, at parties and in shops, what I saw last night and which is my 'favourite programme'. This is infallible as a talking point.

You choose what you like, you are your own critic and auditioner, and you have your own moments of exasperation or sheer loathing of the scene or the people in front of you. You may go for *Call My Bluff* or try to find some suggestion of the genius of Trollope in the dress-display of *The Pallisers*, you may well be intrigued by the ingenuity of *Columbo* or the authenticity of *Z Cars*; I may prefer *University Challenge* (though my mind does not often work quickly enough to defeat the young champions) or Esther Rantzen's exposures of the silliness and crookedness that menaces our daily lives. You watch *Kojak* and *Cannon*; I follow each instalment of *Crown Court* with admiration for the skill of its acting and actuality. I can take the interminable commonplaces of *Coronation Street*, finding it genuinely proletarian, but I can't stand *Crossroads* which seems common and pretentious. You like Cilla Black and *Top of the Pops*; I dislike Jimmy Savile and am not hooked on *The Generation Game*. Every man has his own bad taste, though I for one could not have got through those three months without television.

Yes, I enjoyed looking at television for three months of unbroken rest from any more arduous occupation. It did not give me the ecstatic enjoyment that the London theatre gave me in my early twenties, or the reverent enthusiasm with which I read books by the 'modern' authors whom I worshipped in my 'teens, or the thrill of listening to Beethoven symphonies when, quite late in life, I learned to appreciate them, but it did what I needed most during an illness, it *passed the time*, which was almost all I asked. Nor do I see why great things are not to emerge from television, a new form of drama perhaps or some kind of personal presentation which will do more than satisfy the smirking interviewer, or as yet unpredicted excursions into comedy. I see no promise of greatness in it as yet, but surely the framework is already being formed and our descendants may—if they exist—do with it what the Elizabethans did with the amorphous beginnings of drama, or make the sculpture that the Greeks came to develop from the crudities of cavemen, that is to say, create the greatest within a few decades of the first achievements which never have been and perhaps never can be excelled? If you believe as I do that all forms of art leap suddenly to peaks of fulfilment and then continue on a level of near mediocrity for the rest of time, with a few hillocks of achievement here and there, you will expect a world-shattering genius to arise in the cinema, on television, or in plastic arts, who will drive us to make comparisons with Shakespeare, Beethoven, Michelangelo, rather than shrilly trying to talk of Eliot, Britten or Epstein as though they were artists on the heroic scale. But not yet, of course, not by any means yet, even to the faithful who have hopes of television today. The clowns can split our sides but no one can drive us to tears or make us sit in satisfied meditation long after the wonder on the Box has faded out.

I 'did a lot of thinking', as they say, during those first crippled months, and I use 'thinking' as it is commonly intended, as an occupation like eating or writing. Does anyone really think like this? Set aside a fixed period and turn to it in preference to doing something else? I know I don't and have never been able to do so, perhaps because I have not the makings of another cliché, no 'power of concentration', or perhaps because I have naturally a dragon-fly mind which is never idle but never kept in one place long. In writing I wait for the next thought to come as, thank God, it never fails to do. Even as a novelist I start with only the vaguest knowledge of what may evolve and find this an infinitely less modest disclaimer than it appears to be, because I believe that one of the greatest of the world's novelists, Cervantes, wrote *Don Quixote* by the same instant improvising. Even Sancho Panza may possibly have been an afterthought and I do not think a single one of the episodes was schemed out before the writing began.

However, a fact realized at this time was that every one of the thirty-odd novels I had written had been more than half a failure because I never succeeded in concentrating all of such talents as I possess in a single book, never achieved that sense of fulfilment which must come to a novelist when he is conscious of having forced his 'heart and nerve and sinew' to the colossal task of writing a good story. Not because my books are more or less frivolous, as the best of them, *Exiles*, and *Wolf from the Door*, quite certainly are. Good frivolity takes as much effort to maintain as tragedy, if not more, but because, although I have tried in every case to write the best novel of which I am at the time capable, I have never wholly achieved it and probably do not have it in me to do so. I can make plenty of excuses. When I began to write novels I had no guidance, and as I progressed I had to write too much and too fast to keep pace with a criminal contract which was forced on me by the late Walter Hutchinson. Then, having formed the habit of facile choice of subject, I continued in it till recent years. But these are only excuses, for if I *had* been able to follow the pure light of genius I should have dismissed Hutchinson and all his wiles from my life, while I wrote what I ought to have been able to write in my thirties. A few of my tales should not perhaps be dismissed as worthless and most of them are entertaining, but I have never collected all I possess and thrown it into the writing of one satisfying novel.

But I 'know my place', as domestic servants used to say. I know my place among modern writers and perceive that it depends almost entirely on this sequence of autobiographical books with all their trivialities, prejudices and diversions. If they as a whole do not succeed (in the literary and not material sense), then I have wasted the best part of half a century during which I have wanted very little except to write. I am quite undaunted by the prospect, whichever way it goes, even if the ultimate verdict is one of mediocrity. I have done my best and if the sequence does not come off, now or in the future, I shall at least have kept myself alive by it and richly enjoyed the daily stint of work from 1956 till now. To live twice, once in fact and once in memory, is something given to few of us and I am grateful for it. And if my memory overwhelms fact now that I can *do* so little to provide incident, I am grateful still.

I suppose every writer, if not every creative artist, tries at some time in his later life to sum up what he has or has not achieved, fearlessly to see his place among his contemporaries in the field. Some have openly exaggerated their importance, some have shyly underrated it. Some have given no perceptible thought to it, some have pitied themselves for what they see as lack of recognition. Few have adjudicated their own talents with precision. I do not claim to have done so but am content to leave criticism till, if ever, this series of books appears as one.

I know that my taste in the works of other writers is considered by most people to be eccentric, if not adolescent. Of English novelists I have openly maintained that none has had 'greatness'—again I must use that inexact term—since the 1920s when both Conrad and Hardy died, and only a few (like D. H. Lawrence, perhaps?) have written books which may outlive the noisy ecstasies of modern critics. Poetry died, or at least withered, with the last of the Georgians, and in the theatre we have seen only a series of ephemeral stimulants with no significance or depth. If then my own literary opinions are so generally considered out-of-date, how can I gauge the value or lack of it of my own work? The answer of course is that I cannot do so in any modern sense and that when I say I know my place I only mean that I am aware of what is generally considered my status in the herd of present-day writers. It is not, I hasten to say, an exalted one. No critic gets a rocket from his editor for having ignored a book of mine. But so long as it is sufficient to give me enough borrowers in the lending-libraries to provide me with a living, I do not grumble at my lot. Vanished long since are the towering ambitions, the watchful eye on rivals, the purple passages and the startling ideas which were going to make my next book an overpowering success. Forgotten are the early risings to scan the day's newspapers in search of reviews. Gone—if they ever existed—are the advantageous meetings with other writers or hopeful subscriptions to the Society of Authors, the P.E.N., the Royal Society of Literature and all the rest, not only because I cannot afford them but also because I am not often interested in other writers except perhaps those rare ones who become, for reasons other than literary, my friends.

While spring and summer passed and the year moved towards autumn and the birds on my bird-table grew more varied in species, my thoughts were not in the least bitter, especially when for the first time in my fifty years as a writer I received some recognition of my past professional industry and present predicament in the shape of a grant from the Royal Literary Fund. My publishers had applied three times to the Arts Council for the aid which the committee of this body customarily give to writers who are engaged in unprofitable work which may be of ultimate use to social historians, enumerating the books in this series by which I hoped to complete it. Although this organization had generously helped writers of far less use in this connection than myself, they had flatly refused to help me, so that the grant from the Royal Literary Fund, was doubly welcome to me. As for the repeated promises of successive governments to relieve writers in England of the intolerable weight of providing their work free to the library, and thus to virtually their entire readership, I had long since lost hope of this in my lifetime, though I recognized the heroic work being done by Brigid Brophy and Maureen Duffy and others to bring an end to this monstrous and, one would have thought, self-evident injustice. I found it no more than grotesque that a girl of no great ability, education or experience should earn more by typing a thousand words than an established author earned by writing them, and far more than I could afford to pay my brilliant secretary, with thirty years' experience of my work, for typing and sub-editing it. I accepted this wryly but without repining as the natural reward of a free and interesting life. And after all, I had to admit that throughout it I had put many objectives before material success.

Six

Oxford and Salperton

As the summer of 1974 began to pass I realized that though I should never be able to walk more than a few yards unaided, I could travel by train and car and pony trap, and though the free flow of my vigorous handwriting was lost I could write in letters that Joseph at least could decipher and reproduce. So the 'stroke' had been without the direst consequences and I might even have a decade or so of life in front of me, life that would not be dreary or sour. This made me recall the friends and relatives who had been less lucky than I, since luck for me consists (among other things) of a healthy, unabbreviated life. In particular I thought of three of them, my younger brother Laurie, my lifelong friend Richard Blake Brown, and my successful fellow-writer Louis Golding.

Of the last of them I recall that scarcely one of the earlier of this series was without a chapter devoted to his comically usurious and selfish, yet somehow amiable, character. Ours was a love–hate relationship at its most manifest, and during the last few years of his life I found him frankly unbearable. It was another writer who reported to me in Tangier that the only event that had happened in London which caused more laughter than Louis's wedding was Louis's funeral which followed it by a few months, for he had the gift of extracting publicity from everything that happened to him, even when he made a public event of his marriage to one of the female characters in his book *Magnolia Street*, who in looks and build resembled him closely. Poor Louis! He could never understand why he

74

was not considered to be one of the big best-selling authors like Priestley.

But I missed him, while I was lying there in Bournemouth. If he had lived he would not have come down to see me since gestures of this kind to a friend were unthinkable in his jealous mind. He owed it to his position to regard every visit to anyone as a gracious act of patronage, and never accepted an invitation to dinner unless it included one of his minions. But he would have amused me, cheered me up, answered the telephone with news of his own current books and the small triumphs he was just then claiming. And no one, friend or enemy, and I least of all, could ever call Louis a bore. Is not that sufficient epitaph for any man in this tedious age?

Nor did folk think Richard Blake Brown was a bore, though he was an egomaniac of another kind. I will not recall my friendship with him at Tonbridge School for I have done so already in *The Altar in the Loft*, or the time when we rented neighbouring cottages in the Cotswold village of Salperton, for it is related in *The Wild Hills*, yet I still feel I have failed to do justice to that flamboyant, exhibitionistic, somewhat dishonest yet notably vivacious and memorable man. He had, said Fredric Warburg who was for a short time his publisher, 'he had a tiny talent', and I daresay that was true, though 'tiny' is the last adjective I should apply to Richard, whose clothes, furniture and writings were all vulgarly outsize. Most surprisingly, remembering the irrepressible natural gaiety which he exuded, in the last few years of his life he 'took to drink' and was burned to death after a drunken accident with an oil lamp. To say that I missed him during my months of illness is inaccurate, for after several unpleasant episodes in which I went a long way to visit him and he alcoholically insulted waiters and taxi-drivers, I felt that in his later condition he was *insortable*, but I missed the old Dickie with whom I had played at church services (with vestments made on my mother's sewing machine), with whom I had walked through the meadows to Grantchester when I was staying with him in

Cambridge, whom I had so often seen passing my cottage in the Cotswolds on one of his far-ranging and indefatigable bicycle runs. ('Half-a-crown to the boy with the largest cock!' he used to call to a group of village lads idling through a Sunday afternoon.) He was a rare and individualistic spirit and enlivened many dull natures, another of those beings who are at their best in boyhood and young manhood, and become less likeable in maturity and old age.

I suppose that my brother Laurie was another such, for he too died through excess of alcohol. Born four years after me, he shared much of my early life, riding on the step of my bicycle on my way home from Tonbridge School, sharing confidences of early love-affairs. He had gone up to Oxford and got a half-blue for cross-country running while I was still adventuring in the stews of London. He had joined me in the antiquarian bookshop I had started in Rochester, and together we had pennilessly fought the book-trade for a place in the Ring, and issued a monthly catalogue to the trade to sell back to them at a profit the books we had bought against them. We had attempted to repeat these successes at various times and in several places after that, but once having broken a business partnership we could never mend a personal one.

Laurie joined the Ordnance Corps (not then the R.A.O.C.) in the first week of war, was given his commission before I was, remained in Germany for a year or two afterwards and finally came home to an unambitious life of teaching in preparatory schools for the rest of his days. As he had never taken his degree, he had small chance of advance, and he tried to write but failed after his first novel. Yet throughout he remained almost universally popular and admired. I found it hard to forgive several of his *gaffes*—for instance, his bursting in drunkenly on a conference I was having with Carol Reed, who had commissioned me to write a film script immediately after he had made *The Third Man*. But I remained fond of him even after financial and personal differences, and his blatant failures in loyalty and fraternity.

Of him, truly I can say that during those months I missed him grievously.

Another stroke of good fortune came to me about the time when I could walk as far as I am ever likely to do; good fortune of a kind which the more self-opinionated might call deserved. An undergraduate of Magdalen College, Oxford, announced himself as a fan of my writing, and commenced the exhausting and expensive task of collecting all my books. What is more, he volunteered to spend August in my home, thus enabling Joseph to have a much-needed holiday in India. Michael Holloway, the six-foot son of a broad-minded schoolmaster, was undertaking more than it appears, just as Joseph did when I first had the stroke, but having agreed to it he fulfilled his promise generously and Joseph went by air to Bombay on July 29th, planning to return by August 27th. If ever a holiday was deserved, this short one of Joseph's with the members of his family was amply so, though I doubt if I could have got through the month had it not been for Michael's supremely kind offer.

What was more, he had a small car into which I was able with some difficulty to pack my gammy leg. The first journey I made—and it was also the first out of Bournemouth since I had been sent to bed—was to the New Forest. I had been conscious of the proximity of that region while I remained unable to visit it and I took advantage of Michael's car to go to Alan's house. I liked to think of myself as living 'somewhere near the New Forest' rather than 'in Bournemouth', though I did not openly claim this. But it was through Alan Blond's invitation that I had come to, and discovered a home in, the region, so that the New Forest was rather more than a name to me. It was as lovely now as it had been in spring, for it seems that the Forest responds to all seasons.

Having made that little journey I became bolder and suggested that we should motor to Oxford. With that city I felt even closer ties than with the New Forest, indeed I found it hard to convince myself that I had never been an

77

undergraduate there. That I might have been once, had I not been confined to teaching in preparatory schools or obtained a post in Buenos Aires when I was nineteen years old, was a perpetually sore point in my recollections, but when I went to live in the Cotswolds ten years later I passed through Oxford so frequently that I knew every bookshop, if not every College building in the town. I stayed in St John's College when my brother Laurie was up, and in University College when Barton Wills was. I dined in the St James Restaurant during the years when that was the meeting-place of all the undergraduates of a certain 'set', and travelled long distances to see Laurie come in first in the cross-country events of that time. I remembered Louis Golding, when I was driving him through Oxford to the Cotswolds, being crushed by one of his Cockney charmers to whom he wanted to show his old rooms in Queen's College. 'He can come down and see my college, Peckham Road Elementary School, if he wants to. I don't want to see his.' No wonder Louis did not speak a word for an hour after that. He was so proud of having, against all odds, won a place at the University and taken a brilliant degree there. The boy had been deliberately cruel as Louis, you may think, provoked him to be. But, good heavens, that was in the early 1930s.

On the August day in 1974 which I am remembering, the city had not changed nearly so much as I feared. Bridges and buildings, running water and chiming clocks, it was all much as I remembered it forty years ago. I recalled a theory voiced among Laurie's friends that before the internal combustion engine invaded Oxford it should have been made a walled city, forbidden to all traffic but carts and bicycles, when it could have kept sacred its dreaming spires. Youthful and impractical, of course, but to one like me who had missed most of the gifts that Oxford had to bestow, a theory with considerable attraction.

The undergraduates, Michael told me, perhaps because fewer of them came from public schools, were more class-conscious, more anxious to be considered gentlemen, than the young men of old, perhaps even more than in my brother Laurie's day. Then the leading figures had been his friends Graham Eyres-Monsell, Gavin Faringdon, Arthur Waters-Welch and others who dined nightly at the George and, conscious that their lordly status in the University was unassailable, created their legends, like Harold Acton immediately before them, without need of their genealogical notability.

After an evening spent in several Oxford bars, we set out on the Sunday morning for Salperton, the lonely village of some fifty inhabitants off the main road to Cheltenham. Here I had lived in a little Elizabethan workman's cottage for the years between 1931 and 1936, and although I had never revisited it I felt it to be—of all villages in England— the one I should be most likely to haunt after death, if my dog Dingo, my goat Faustine and my peacocks Guy and Pauline could accompany me from the Shades.

Yet the road from Oxford brought back not the innumer- able motor journeys along it, not the tollgate at which I had to halt, not even my brother Laurie or my friend Richard Blake Brown who had so often accompanied me, but associations which pre-dated all these and went back to my first feverishly excited reading of *Sinister Street*. That reading had been done on a school holiday at my home in East- bourne in 1917, and the experience has never been forgotten. When I sold all my books with most of my other possessions in 1972 I kept my two volumes of the first edition of this, inscribed as they were by Monty Mackenzie, and I am not ashamed to admit that I read this now unfashionable masterpiece every few years or so, along with Conrad's *Lord Jim*.

Why, in returning to Oxford and the Cotswolds in 1974, I should have thought more about Monty and his books than of my own living in Salperton I find it hard to explain, but I know that Laurie was as much a devotee of Mackenzie as I was in those days, and that while he was up at Oxford he had visited Burford (not then a second-hand furniture mart) and identified Plasher's Mead among its houses. I know, too, that when I was to receive the first sizeable sum of money from writing, for the film rights of *Cosmopolis* which Carl Laemmle (of Universal) had bought and subsequently reneged on, Laurie advised me to look somewhere west of Oxford in 'the fresh green lap of fair King Richard's land,' and it was with Laurie that I had nearly rented a house in Burford and after that found The Long House in Salperton where I had settled for five Theocritan years.

I had not yet met Monty Mackenzie at that time but he and his prose informed all my travels from Oxford, eastward to the limit of a day's cycling from Oxford in the west. I had called my pair of peacocks Guy and Pauline, and never passed the Cotswold Gateway on the London road without remembering that in the small town down the slope, Mackenzie himself had lived, as he caused Guy and Pauline to do in his book. It was indeed a rural and barebacked country of hills and fine churches and people who spoke with the dialect of Gloucestershire.

Returning to it we passed with horror through the *marché aux puces* of Burford and found that the road from there to Northleach, though more loaded with traffic, was as unpopulated in its surroundings as ever. In Northleach I did not stop at the Union Hotel, for since my stroke my dart-playing arm was useless, but at the service station on its outskirts, which had faced the old prison buildings, I stopped to enquire for the two industrious young brothers who had owned it. So close did I seem to those days when I had bought two second-hand cars from them and considered them my friends that I was not surprised to hear that Mr Webb and his partner were still in charge, though they had gone out some minutes ago. It was not till I was driving on past Hangman's Corner, where the last man hanged for sheep-stealing had swayed in the wind a century and a half ago, that I realized that the brothers must now be in their late sixties and that their being still the working owners of the place was almost a miracle.

Farther on I found the tree-lined way to Salperton which

left the main road at a cottage which in my time—I remembered hearing—housed a farm labourer with seven children who earned 25/- a week. It seemed farther than I remembered it from the main road to the village but its few little houses were still grouped round the stream which had run through my orchard. The Long House had scarcely changed, though the orchard had been stripped of its aged fruit trees at the bark of which Faustine, the nanny-goat, had nibbled, while hideous new conifers had been planted in their place. Worse than that, the great walnut tree whose unripened nuts Mrs Smith the postmistress had pickled for me had been cut down—why, God knows—and the green slope behind the house remained uncultivated. Teddy Ashford, I remember, a school friend of Wrekin days and a successful architect, had suggested that perennials should be planted to fight their way through the grass, and I had always intended to do this, but somehow it had 'never got done' by me or by the succeeding owners. But here it was, the road between Cotswold walls along which I had accelerated in the red Lea-Francis on my way home, while Dingo my yellow Alsatian could recognize the sound of its engine three miles away, so I had been told by Eric Harwood the village baker's son who worked for me.

It was not that I needed to come here to remember these things, indeed I daresay I had a clearer picture of them in Tangier where I wrote *The Wild Hills* than now when I saw only the actual picture of them. It was, in fact, the differences between the Salperton I knew so intimately forty years before and the Salperton I stared at now. And not a living soul, I was told in answer to enquiries, was common to the two of them. In the interim between I had learned by chance in reading *The Letters of Oscar Wilde* that the father of our 'Squire' (Hatfield Harter), whose name I knew was George Lloyd Foster Harter, had been a friend of Wilde's at Magdalen, a curious little detail of that family tree. But now they were all gone, Hatfield Harter, his mother, his cousin Admiral Salmon and the servants they had employed, and the mixed architecture of their tree-surrounded house. The house had become an institution of some kind and none of the cottages housed the inhabitants of my time or their families. But it was with an odd sensation of having returned to a vanished past that down in the village I saw the home I had loved.

Back in Bournemouth I decided to go up to London, realizing that even the phrase sounds dated to all but the most conservative commuters of today. My father and those of his generation always talked of 'running up to town' and 'going down to the country' but I have been reproved by younger folk for using such archaic terms today. Nor did I have the same pleasure in the thought of London as I had when I came home from Tangier to visit it. I have come to the conclusion that great old cities are for youth, and younger more provincial ones for the aged. It was not only that in London at that time I could not move about except by Michael's car or a taxi; it was that the whole tempo of London was not for a lame man, or even for an ageing one. Only five years ago I had always been able to telephone successfully the taxi rank in Little Venice, now it might answer immediately, which meant I would be early for an appointment, or after twenty minutes, or not at all. In Paris and Madrid, or Cologne or Buenos Aires for that matter, I knew that I would be faced with the same difficulties, the price of living in a great metropolis. However, on this occasion I would be driven by car as surely as I had driven myself in the last car I had owned, a Renault Frégate. To think that when I was last living in London I had flitted about, parking my Opel almost wherever I chose, and had never heard of traffic wardens, or car-park attendants as many of my contemporaries insisted on calling them. Yet another case of *Eheu Fugaces*—and that was becoming my most habitual Latin quotation.

But the weather was pleasant and I called first at the beautiful home of Beverley Nichols at Ham Common. He too had been struck down by an illness far graver than mine in its suffering but of less consequence in its effects, since he could still drive his car about London. I found him as cheerful as an old Forsyte, and far more youthful and entertaining. Two of the acquaintances who had given us most prodigious amusement, most ribald laughter, Godfrey Winn and Louis Golding, were now no more, and we had to make do with laughing-stocks less extravagantly absurd, but they were not hard to find, chiefly among politicians in this ridiculous age.

We walked round the garden, the smallest and most perfect among those open to the public for charity, then came in to eat a crab *mousse* which, though Beverley claims not to be a cook, was superb. Michael produced an attaché-case full of Beverley's books for him to sign, an inescapable habit of his when he meets any writer of reputation, and with cheerful good wishes for our mutual recovery we parted and Michael drove me to Little Venice.

It was the first time in the twenty-odd years that I had become a friend of Patrick Kinross that I had been to his house without luggage, since during my Mediterranean years I had always come from abroad to take advantage of his generous hospitality for a week, a fortnight, sometimes a month's stay in London. He too had gone through an operation but showed no signs of it—indeed I thought Patrick became more himself, more a healthy-looking elderly Scottish peer as he aged. He had not changed noticeably since he had visited me twenty years ago in prison and by his humour and encouragement taught me to regard that episode of scandalous injustice and malice as a joke in bad taste. Indeed, was he not to write in a review of a book of mine about Tangier? 'Here the smarties lived on the Mountain—a "little suburban monticle", as Mr Croft-Cooke sees it—in spacious villas with competitive and well-tended gardens. The sleazies lived down by the docks or in the Moroccan Bazaar. The in-betweens lived in between, comfortably accessible to either, in the town itself. Rupert Croft-Cooke had the best of both these worlds. He was in the fortunate position of having lately spent some months in Wormwood Scrubs, for an irregularity of behaviour no longer pronounced illegal or considered remotely disreputable. This gave him, to his inestimable literary advantage, the admission, denied to less fortunate authors, into an exclusive society of criminals, whom he would not otherwise have been privileged to meet. Thus here he was in middle age, blessed with a rich new source of experience and the material for six more novels. These, together with ten more volumes of autobiography, he settled down happily to write, in a Tangerine flat, observing with his eyes and tape-recording with his mind the mixed goings-on and malicious name-dropping chatter in the cosmopolitan bars around him, then transferring it into print with appropriate candour and indiscretion.' To Patrick it really was an 'inestimable literary advantage' to have known the screwsmen and villains of Wormwood Scrubs, and any small loss in reputation which had befallen me as the *bourgeois* good citizen I had tried to be was negligible compared with it. How grateful then I had been for his friendship at that time and since.

He autographed the books which Michael brought out of his capacious brief-case and asked a few questions about present-day Oxford and offered us the Highland Malt whisky, which like his friend and mine, the late Monty Mackenzie, he drank in preference to other spirits.

But I had another call to make in London, for I had taken my work to a new agent. Only a jobbing writer will realize how important this is to a man who is dependent solely on his writing to make a living. Since I earned my first little cheques from periodicals in my 'teens I have employed no less than half-a-dozen firms of agents, starting with A. M. Heath in the days when Audrey Heath herself ruled the agency, and when John Rothenstein (later to become Director of the Tate Gallery) represented her and successfully sold articles of mine to the *Sunday Express*. Then for a long mixed period I went to Curtis Brown in London (not to be confused with Curtis Brown, New York) but left it out of antipathy for the younger son of the original Curtis Brown who I believed mishandled some important negotiations for me. I was bitter about that. Also I liked other members of the staff at Curtis Brown's offices which were then in Covent Garden—Juliet O'Hea, Graham Watson, Dorothy Daly who brilliantly sold my serial rights and the 'character' in charge of the office, who had been with the firm since he had been batman in the First World War to the exceedingly promising first son of old Curtis Brown, who had been killed, tragically for everyone concerned, particularly for the firm's authors.

So I returned to the care of A. M. Heath and Company, now (1955) directed by Cyrus Brooks, and remained with them until I was inveigled by A. D. Peters (who was on a visit to Tangier) to become one of his authors. This was all very well until I realized that Peters himself was past active management, and when John Montgomery, who had sold a film of mine, left the firm, so did I, and went for the third time to A. M. Heath. I feel sure I should have remained with them for the rest of my literary life had it not been for differences—with one of the partners.

It was Beverley Nichols who recommended me to go to Eric Glass, and there could not have been a better agent for him and for commercially successful authors like him, but not for me, since I give an agent a great deal of work in several different departments and grumble when small possibilities are not followed up. Had I been about to produce a best-selling novel or a 'natural' of a West End play, I am sure Eric Glass would have made me a rich man. As it is, he did well for me by the agreements he negotiated on my behalf, but he did not feel that his staff had the time to cope with my many demands.

So it was now, after a great deal of thought and discussion, that I had asked John McLaughlin (of Campbell, Thomson & McLaughlin) to see what he could do with my work. It will seem from these confessions that I have been a difficult, not to say exigent, author for an agent to deal with, and I daresay that is true. Certainly I have written far too much and, like Hilaire Belloc in the rhyme, seem to think that 'nobody minds All his books being of different kinds'. On the other hand I never miss a chance of advising young authors to find a good agent and remain loyal to him or her, for to try to make a living without an agent is like trying to go to law without a solicitor. This is the sort of pompous statement I am entitled to make after publishing several million words since boyhood. The statement, moreover, is true, as any writer will tell you, from a scribbler of children's rhymes to the kind of successful novelist who keeps half an eye on the current needs of film or television producers.

So I lunched with John McLaughlin and at once found him an agent after my own heart, not too grand to deal with minor pieces of writing, but interested in handling anything big that might come along. I signed a contract and have certainly never regretted it. A writer's livelihood depends at whatever age he has reached and whatever success he may have attained on publishers and agents, and it may be seen that I have dealt with a number of them both in England, America, Europe, South America and India. I consider myself something of an authority on their ways and have gladly offered my advice to young writers. Most of them in both categories are honest and competent, but God help the writer who gets landed with a fool or a crook. My system has been to seek my publisher's advice about an agent, and an agent's about a publisher. It works.

Seven

Conduct Unbecoming

A senseless rigmarole had become popular during the General Election of that year which proclaimed: 'Vote! Vote Right, Vote Left, Vote middling but VOTE! It is your duty as a citizen and by voting you will help your country! Not to vote is to be lazy, spineless and cowardly!' Nothing could be sillier than this gabble which was mounted everywhere with the mock-wisdom of sophistry, and I ignored it.

But in doing so, I realized with some annoyance, I had made a decision on one political issue, if it was only to find that Heath and Wilson, or Conservatism and Socialism as they were understood then, were equally antipathetic to me, or equally ridiculous if you find the word more honest. But this had always been so. I have a gift, nothing less, for putting myself on the side in an argument most unpopular with those around me, my parents, my friends, my associates. As an adolescent, without understanding the term, I called myself a Socialist, infuriating my dear father and rousing the anger of the young men who taught with me in preparatory schools, those hotbeds of class-consciousness. By the time I started writing and met Left-wingers in Charles Lahr's bookshop and other places, I found the Left opinionated and shabby in thought and appearance, yet I was, I remember, passionately 'on the side of the miners' in the General Strike, in spite of my undergraduate brother's enthusiasm for train-driving.

I think now that it needed some issue on which I had a little knowledge and strong feeling to rouse me to any political opinion at all. I was not 'pro-Franco' in the Spanish

Civil War but I knew enough of the country and its people to make the prediction, so unpopular in England, that a victory for the Nationalists would be the best result for Spain and for the rest of Europe, as indeed it has proved to be. The best for us, for the allies for that matter, since Franco, it should be remembered, was the only European head of state to stand up to the bullying tactics of Hitler when the crunch came. People are fond of remembering that Hitler sent aid and armaments to Franco in his struggle against the Russian-aided Government supporters. They are less concerned with Franco's wily refusal to let the Nazis march through Spain to North Africa, knowing that if he had agreed, the course of the war would have been very different and less advantageous to us. 'Of course', Franco is said to have bluffed, 'I cannot prevent you, but I must tell you that I could not hold the Army back from opposing you if you started to cross the Pyrenees.' That, and Franco's paying of pensions to most professional soldiers and to all Civil Guards *whichever side they had fought on* is rarely remembered by the supporters of Negrin. These are more ready to think of Englishmen who have been able to see the benefits of Franco's Spain as Fascists, pro-Nazis, traitors and murderers, and to consider all soldiers who fought in the Civil War as cowards and assassins if they were not of that minority that claimed to be fighting for a 'Legitimate Government' long after any semblance of it had disappeared. Franco and his policies have created a prosperous middle- and working-class in Spain, and isn't that what all Socialists (or Communists for that matter) aim everywhere to do?

Other issues that have roused me in the past have been the Abdication—chiefly from a detestation of Baldwin and Archbishop Lang—the Liberation of India and Africa, the retention of Gibraltar and a few more treacherously unfulfilled promises like P.L.R.

But there was nothing to excite my sympathy or even interest in what was evident in politics today. Who *cared* whether Wilson replaced Heath or vice-versa? Who cared what Tony Benn or Margaret Thatcher or Denis Healey said? It all came to the same thing and very few if any of us, the voting public, were competent to judge the merits of the issue.

One or two of these in years after 1974 would provide us with riotous occasions for humour, like the Sex Discrimination Act. To me it is frankly incredible that a government—it might have been from any of the parties—should try to earn votes by pandering to a few women demanding a biological change, not in washing-powder but in mankind itself, should try to introduce new pronouns and new occupations totally inappropriate to men and women. It will take only a few years to see the absurdity of this, and Women's Lib will be as dead as ducking to test the abilities of witches. Meanwhile, let those of us with any sense of humour left after those years of depression, enjoy it while we can.

This attitude of rather hostile escape from all political issues has, of course, done me irreparable harm materially as a writer if not artistically as a practician of any of the arts. These are so ill-rewarded both in prestige and material success that almost no man can work alone in them, certainly at the start of his career. The Squirearchy, the apostles of T. S. Eliot, the Spender and Auden clique, the more genuine Leftists who met in Charles Lahr's shop, contributors to periodicals edited by Middleton Murry, John Lehmann, Cyril Connolly, and G. K. Chesterton and his Distributists, all these represented politico-literary schools of a kind, just as Conservatism and Labourite Socialism represented categorically political parties. But I have never been able to sign on with any of them, so that now in my seventies, returning to England after two decades abroad, I was without fellow-believers in anything much at all. There have been times when I have regretted this, when I have longed to be one of a crowd, any crowd, who hold beliefs, enthusiasms or angers in common, when I believed that if I could see the right banner I would march under it. But to seek a cause worth serving is a vain and lonely quest and I have long since ceased to follow it. Only let me write the best book of which I am capable, for so far as I am concerned 'this is the whole duty of man'.

Without that, without that one object in life, mine would have been a pretty useless time to have spent on earth, without a political creed and with only a muddled and uncertain religious one, without a single aim in sight except the unceasing effort to gain experiences and make use of them. A failure at money-making and fame for lack of sufficient purpose to achieve them, here I was passing three score years and ten with a name that meant nothing except to a few eccentric bibliophiles or pilots of voyages of discovery on the lending library shelves, as I had myself been once, unearthing the novels of Arthur Machen and Maurice Hewlett. It was not, I had to admit, a very impressive record and the fact that I had passed an immensely happy life, full of variety, travel, friendship, industry and humour would not seem to many people an adequate recompense for it. But this is beginning to sound like epigraphy and I am not by any means ready for such writing yet. I have become misled by the tatty subject of politics and must now return to happier matters.

Joseph arrived by air, reaching home at midnight on August 27th, having left Bombay on the previous morning. When I thought of my journeys to and from India, two during the war in troopships and two after the war in comfort by ships of the Anchor Line, it seemed that his journey was insignificant except in expense. I remembered the cockroaches endured for weeks between Mombasa and Bombay, the insulting discomfort of the 'dry' and overcrowded ship in which I travelled home to Liverpool in 1946, the traditional aspects of a journey East of Suez in peacetime—scrambling by pretentious passengers for a seat at the Captain's table, deck quoits and the fancy-dress party. I have always been happy on ships and bored in the air, but I sympathized with Joseph who could not leave me for more than four weeks, which were only just sufficient to make visits to his multitudinous family.

Both his father and mother had died in their nineties but

enough of his relatives were left to come down to Bombay in a large party to see him off. They were Tamilians and to those who know India this means that they are from the southern and more intelligent part of the Indian population. They were also Catholics, their ancestors having been converted by St Francis Xavier who lies buried among them in Goa. I am always uncertain how much of the talent with which Joseph edits and types my books and deals with all 'business' problems is due to his race and how much is owed to his long residence in Europe. He probably speaks English better than Tamil, but in which language his own most secret thoughts are expressed I cannot say. He is in some ways a hidebound Englishman, in humour, idiom and ideas. He votes Conservative, goes to an English Mass on Sundays and watches cricket. But surely the manner in which he gets his own way on my behalf with recalcitrant publishers or editors is truly Indian and comes (as I have written elsewhere) from his ability to best the cloth-sellers in Delhi's Chandri Chowk. I was delighted to see him back and not only because I could sleep later in the morning, as I found myself apt to do since my stroke, contrary to my invariable custom in the past.

He gave me news of all his relations, knowing that to me they are a kind of second family. His elder brother Anthony, who had been killed while cycling home from work by a hit-and-run motorist, had left five sons, one of whom was training to be a priest but the others, and Anthony's widow, were not the most favourite members of the family in Joseph's eyes. Anthony had been a schoolmaster. Joseph's second brother Arokiaswamy was a sacristan in a Jesuit college. He also has had seven children and Joseph has helped to provide the marriage portion and wedding expenses for the girls, so important and so expensive in all Indian families. Joseph's one (of three) surviving sister Gracey, whom I remember as a little girl dancing in and out of the house in her sari while I was still in the Army, is married to a railway official and has a fine family of her own. Then there is Joseph's brother-in-law, husband of his late sister Adakaran, who came to say goodbye to Joseph when he was leaving for England with me but unhappily died soon after. She had two sons, one a fine young man named Peter who is Joseph's nephew. Peter too is married and has children as well as a number of nephews and nieces, his wife coming from a large family. So in India I have 'god-children' whom I cannot clearly enumerate. But it is comforting that I have these in addition to my three real godchildren, Richard Hitchcock, Derek Cooke, my brother Geoffrey's son, and Lavinia, daughter of my Anglo-Chinese friend from before the war, Clifford Gibbs. Of this last I shall have more to relate. Not a bad total, I feel, for an elderly bachelor.

I have mourned with Joseph as the news of each loss reached him in England or Morocco, first his elder sister Adakaran, then his gentle old mother who had so often welcomed me with the Madrassi meal in her house, then his sister Pakian who seemed to spend her life knitting adroitly, then Joseph's frail nonagenarian father who used to tell me stories of British officers whom he had known, several of whom, I calculated, must have been commissioned in Queen Victoria's reign. Last of all Joseph had lost his brother Anthony while he himself was staying at his home. I follow, from Joseph's account, the progress of each member of this widespread family as though they were my own, for although India seems to me far away in distance I never feel that in other senses it is remote.

But in another way I found that on his return, and after those months of looking after me as an invalid, Joseph could go out now and so brought me in touch with another collection of young people, for he could do what I could not at this time—though as I have related I had done it all my life—that is make friends with the boys and girls, late teenagers and adolescents who made a habit of meeting in a certain pub. I have often observed with some curiosity how such congregations form, particularly among the young. I can understand that elderly men come to a certain bar for conversation, knowing that they will meet other men and exchange views of the weather, football, politics or notable murders, but for the young one must suppose a liking for beer, an ability to endure, even to *like* the din of a juke-box, a love of chatter for chatter's sake and a chance to meet the girl or boy of their taste. With these they seem content to come night after night to this or that rendezvous, even having to travel long distances to reach it. That which Joseph started patronizing was called The Clarendon; it was in fact one of several separate bars under one roof. All of them were nineteenth century in name and decoration, one of them actually being called The Victoria, but in each was a different clientèle. One might be considered a family bar, full of holiday-makers with their wives meeting and joining in conversation with other holiday-makers. Another was for young couples to sit in earnest conversation, perhaps to engage in curious clinging movements towards closer proximity. The Clarendon was more heterogeneous than the others, hard-drinking, sometimes quarrelsome, classless and for the most part friendly. Its miscellaneous customers welcomed Joseph in their midst as I had seen so many groups of many nationalities welcome him in other countries as well as this. Most of the young men had girls with whom they were 'going' more or less seriously, but for talking they preferred their own sex as they had much more in common with men. I got to know them all, since Joseph would ask them back with their girls for a drink and a curry, both of which they enjoyed. They were noisy except when Joseph told them I was asleep in the next room, when they were extraordinarily considerate.

I came to like most of them though I found it difficult, as it seemed they themselves did, to talk to their girls who were not so much shy as unable to converse in any cogent sense. I decided that I simply did not know and could not guess what young girls talk about among themselves or with their boyfriends—certainly with me they were as dumb as I was. But I enjoyed the company of these young people and a good deal of their music, and came to feel at one with them as I have done with youth all my life, on the dart-boards of pre-war pubs, in the mess and barracks of the Army, in Tangier, Spain and Ireland, wherever I have been in fact. There was a lively young man of gypsy parentage called Paul with a girl who seemed to last longer than almost any of their friends, there were three with the first name of Steve who had nothing in common except their girlfriends whom they passed around: 'Tall Steve', 'Butcher Steve' and 'Birmingham Steve'. There was a good-natured bearded Anglo-Welsh young man named Gerry who loved his pint of beer more than anything else in life but never became drunk on it; there was a public-school type named Mark who was engaged to a Scandinavian girl and another, David, who had actually married one. There was an ex-soldier whose passion was the evening paper which he would read from the first paragraph to the last. Moreover there were barmen, managers, 'bar-persons' as we are asked to call them, and a few elderly eccentrics who came from time to time. In all, an interesting and motley collection whom Joseph brought home just often enough to make me feel I knew them and all their quirks. So this gave to the stolidity of Bournemouth a new enlivenment.

Just as I was beginning to be able to form letters sufficiently well for Joseph to type them—a lengthy process for each of us—Jeffrey Simmons my publisher telephoned to say that he had purchased the book rights of a play which had been successful and was now to be made into a film. Could I undertake to write the novel which was to be published as a hardback and as a paperback by the two appropriate departments of his firm, W. H. Allen? It would have to be completed in three months. Because of my disability I hesitated, but when he told me that the setting was an Indian Army Mess I liked the idea, though I still was not sure that I ought to entertain it. In other days I might have been known, like T. W. H. Crosland, as a 'Jobbing Writer —Estimates Given', and not regarding it as writing in any real sense, I earned a reputation for being able to turn out anything at any notice however brief, which had more than once led to some interesting work. But now with a disabled right hand to add to my difficulties I had doubts of myself.

Jeffrey however suggested that I should come up to London and see the film, which had been completed all but for the Indian sequences, and an offer was made to send a taxi down to Bournemouth to fetch me and take me back.

This was the sort of treatment I had only received in connection with films and I agreed to come to a showing of *Conduct Unbecoming* that week. I took Joseph not only because I was uncertain of being able to move about alone but because as an Indian he would be able to pick out technical details and points of language. It was a rough December morning when we began to run up the A30 and we lunched at the Café Royal before reaching John Mc-Laughlin's office for a preliminary discussion with him and the head of W. H. Allen's paperback subsidiary, Star Books, who was named picturesquely Piers Dudgeon.

Later we went to the little private studio where the film was to be shown and settled down in the back row.

The film began and I quickly realized that whatever skills the original playwright, or the scriptwriter or the director, possessed, they knew little about the India I remembered, still less of an officers' mess such as I had known when I was commissioned in the Third (Queen Alexandra's Own) Gurkha Rifles, and though the film was set in the 1870s the *modus vivendi* had changed little from then to 1943, when I was there. I realized, too, that to make a novel from the film script instead of vice-versa as I had hitherto been accustomed to doing, would be simplicity itself, and before I left London I signed a contract to carry it out. It had an ingenious plot, somewhere between a who-dunnit and a ghost story with some quite good conventional characterization thrown in. I quite looked forward to working on it since the terms were generous and Joseph had already seen Indian details to be amended.

I did not, as I have explained, regard this as creative writing, keeping that ambiguous term for novels or poetry of my own making, but I like to feel that I can turn my hand to most things and recognize that no writing is wholly creative and none is entirely uncreative. It was after all many years since I had written purple passages and read them over to myself full of satisfaction, and it may well be that ability to turn out a competent job in such circumstances is as important as to create. While presenting a number of new characters, I used the dialogue of the original film script, which was excellent, as freely as I wanted, this being a condition on which the contract had been agreed. When *Conduct Unbecoming* appeared as a book under my name 'Now a Major Film. Screenplay by Robert Enders based on the play by Barry England' it would have taken a clever man to work out just who was responsible for what. But I was in no way ashamed of the result.

This was the only work I did during this year because for me 'inability to write' means inability in the physical as well as the literary or metaphorical sense, since all my life I have written in handwriting everything that has been published subsequently, as well as correspondence and miscellaneous wordage. Perhaps this came partly from the fact that when he first came to me Joseph wrote in Tamil calligraphy to his parents and would have found it difficult or impossible to master shorthand, or perhaps it has been from the love of actual physical writing, running across lines of paper with my own words. That year was the first time I had ever been unable to do this in my own free-flowing hand-writing and to communicate slowly with an awkward script was a pain and a labour to me. However, somehow I got it done and very quickly afterwards the novel was printed in paperback and hardback editions and sold in a headlong way.

This task, however, reminds me of another of which I am in no way proud. Readers of earlier books in this series will remember the character of Louis Golding. I did not caricature him—indeed I don't think it would be possible to do so—but I showed him in all his monstrous absurdity and egocentricity. The truth is that for a number of reasons which are not hard to guess no communication passed between us during the last ten years of his life, and although

I kept the little portraits I had of him till I wrote three books which they considerably enlivened, Louis had taken advantage of a misfortune of mine to abuse me rather meanly to the few friends we had in common. All very petty, you will say, and you are right, but perhaps no two persons can be more malicious than a pair of writers, having the means to be so ready at their hands. I laughed unrestrainedly at Louis, he viciously maligned me. And so on for several years until I heard from an agent that Louis had written a novel, unfinished when he died, which his executors were anxious to have finished and published. I knew when I received the typescript that it had been sent to several writers—one of them had in fact accidentally left a letter adressed to him between its pages—and all of them had turned down the opportunity of doing the work of completion. I never had any great opinion of Louis's literary ability and although he had written a bestseller in *Magnolia Street* I had heard the opinion expressed that Victor Gollancz himself was the publishing genius who had brought this about. The uncompleted novel seemed to me an Edwardian effort, one of those books with a tricky plot which a lesser Conan Doyle, E. W. Hornung, Anstey or W. W. Jacobs might have written, with a staleness of idea and setting which foredoomed it to obscurity in the present decade. Should I do it? Poor dear Louis would writhe in his grave if he knew that I was contemplating it, but on the other hand it seemed rather a shame that his last piece of writing should be lost and that the beneficiaries of his will should not be given the fruits of the work he did during his last months. As they had been for Louis himself during all the time I had known him, my feelings now were mixed. I could feel him scribbling away at the thing, sense his moments of satisfaction and of doubt, and could guess what finale he meant to write. In the end I agreed to do it, stipulating that my name should not appear, and the measure of my success or failure can be judged by the reader if he can distinguish the point at which Louis's book ends and mine begins.

It may be guessed that it writing this series of books

claiming familiarity with people and places in the past I receive a large number of letters from readers writing for no better reason than that they too have vivid memories of the place or person, and they wish to share them with me. These are friendly and sometimes interesting letters but I cannot afford to answer more than one or two of them. When I say I 'cannot afford' I speak the literal truth because the meanest little answer entails (i) my time and energy, (ii) Joseph's, plus use of typewriter, (iii) stationery, (iv) stamps, a total reckoned conservatively of 50p a time, and if I write a longer letter I calculate that it costs me a minimum of a pound. This may be considered a mean and usurious way of thinking but the earnings of a professional writer are meanly and usuriously allowed and he is called upon to lend his books to all the world free of charge. To add to his expenses the cost of answering letters from anyone who chooses to write to him, out of curiosity or for the collection of autographs, is just too much. However, he can't do anything as simple as destroy them all unread because just here and there is a letter which demands an answer, and now and then information turns up which is helpful or a request to supply facts which only I can give.

These latter are usually from biographers, or would-be biographers of someone mentioned in a book of mine. Of such were two enquiries which I received about this time and in both cases I answered the letter willingly and invited the sender to call on me. One was from a young man who lived or worked in South Africa and was planning a book on my dear old friend, counsellor in my boyhood, Douglas Blackburn, and the other was from a young man who had been commissioned to write a book about John Lodwick.

I was delighted to hear that old Douglas Blackburn was still a name in South Africa and that his books *Prinsloo of Prinsloosdorp* and the rest were still read. Few if any of the men who had stood round him in the bar of The Rose and Crown in Tonbridge and listened to his never-ending repertoire of adventure stories could recall him now, I judged, though I could remember everything he said to me and my father sitting under the trees in the garden of Cage House during the First World War, while the thudding of guns was audible from across the Channel. A great man, Douglas Blackburn, and I hoped my enquiring friend would do him justice.

A writer of a very different kind was John Lodwick who was killed in a car accident with his Catalan publisher Josef Janes. His future biographer knew more about him and his crazy inconstancy and wild kindness and hospitality than I did, but we agreed in thinking his first book, *Peal of Ordnance*, was his best. His novels had never quite 'come off' though he had tried again and again to bring theme and execution together to make a really good book. John was hopelessly volatile and uncertain of his aims as a writer, he was also erratic and sometimes offensive as a man, but he was greatly loved and missed by his few friends and the women in his life when he was killed. I was glad to hear news of his last wife Micaela and of his children, and to know that he was to be made the subject of a biography, and I did what little I could to help the biographer.

Eight

Travel

It will seem that I was beginning to accustom myself to a less eventful life than I had been used to, since Bournemouth does not *sound* very exciting. But I had, gratefully, the gift of turning dull surroundings and duller people into colourful and interesting ones, perhaps because I despise those who call others bores when they have not taken the trouble to draw out what is worthwhile and generous in their minds. So it was now that somehow Joseph and I had added to our intimate acquaintance the young man David to whom I have already referred, his Swedish wife Lene and their baby son Dominic. A conventional trio, you think? Well, yes, and no.

David was not in fact an orphan—he had a father living somewhere in the North of England, but no mother, brothers or sisters. There was also, or had lately been, a grandfather of whom he spoke with immense admiration and respect, his first tutor in the bucolic arts, a mighty man of valour and one of the few older people to whom David would admit respect. David was not a drifter; he could work skilfully and ambitiously at what interested him— chiefly seamanship and catering. Though entirely virile, he was blessed or cursed with a face so beautifully shaped and a skin so notably clear that he was stared after in the street. Lene too had the fair skin and light gold hair of a healthy Scandinavian girl, while Dominic made conquests wherever he turned.

David was aware of all this, disgusted at himself and his appearance in some ways but humorously conscious of it in others. He was twenty-seven and knew that he could be mistaken for a teenaged ballet-dancer. But the passions of his life were simple, his little son and the shooting of wild animals, always provided that the creatures shot were edible. I have noticed this before among people who shoot and hunt and fish; any opprobrium they feel their sports merit is quickly absolved so long as the game, however improbably, can be eaten or may be considered to rid the farmer of a pest. This does not make much logic for me since I have a natural fastidiousness which makes me dislike killing any living thing, even creeping or stinging insects. I would not go as far as the Jain sect of Hindus who wear a veil over their mouths for fear of demolishing by their breath a gnat or midge, but I feel distaste even for stamping on a noxious insect. This does not, however, make me loath to eat with enjoyment fish, shellfish, birds or ground game. It is for me a matter not of ethics or morals but of taste— or distaste in most cases.

Now it happened that another young man was paying too much attention to Lene and was foolish enough to brag about it while David was cutting up meat for the dog. The sequel was foreseeable and tiresome. David pinked the interloper in the arm, meaning only—he swore to me privately and to the Crown Court before which he was brought publicly—that his intention was only to scare or at the most threaten the young man, but sequels have a habit of accumulating, and David was remanded for several weeks on a charge of A.B.H. His wife returned to Sweden, taking his son, while the 'rival' did what rivals are supposed to do on these occasions, 'escaped abroad'.

When the police, who maintained an admirably detached attitude to the whole affair, brought David up to be remanded, he was given bail which I stood for him. It was interesting to watch the struggle between his natural feelings and polite expression of gratitude and the adolescent pride (or is it arrogance?) so common among the young generation who cannot escape a decent sense of obligation, especially to older men, but hate themselves for feeling it.

However, he appeared in Court on the day fixed and, there being no witnesses now that the 'rival' had disappeared, he was remanded on bail again while a further search was made —equally in vain, fortunately for David, and at last he was free to go.

It was now that his adventures became interesting to me. Fights, even with knives, were so commonplace in Tangier (and indeed almost everywhere else in this century) that I was not greatly intrigued by an account of one, but when David set off with the idea of making for Sweden, where his wife and son lived and where he had served in the Swedish Merchant Fleet and was a paid-up member of the Swedish seamen's union, then I wanted to hear his account of things. It was so like my own wayfaring in my teens and twenties that it brought to my cosy little home in Bournemouth a breath of much that I had missed in the last few decades.

It made me review my own claims to be a traveller. I have stated these elsewhere but they will serve to show what it meant to me in 1975 to have a young man, of about the age at which I had done most of my necessitous travel, coming to me when he first came back to Bournemouth and recounting his adventures. For I had been where he had, in more senses than one.

During a train journey between Cheltenham and London a man once told me his life-story. It was not sensational and he had no dramatic gifts, but it aroused a very sincere sympathy from me. He had gone into his father's well established business as a young man, and because his father had died soon afterwards, he had taken over its direction and responsibilities at an earlier age than had been anticipated. Now, approaching sixty, he had decided to retire. He would be in comfortable circumstances for the rest of his life.

'And what will you do when you retire?' I asked him.

He answered without a moment's hesitation—'I shall travel.'

'Have you never done so?'

'Oh, I've spent holidays in France and Switzerland. But I mean travel—see the world.'

I never saw him again but I should like to know how he fared. For I do not believe that such travelling merits the name. Galsworthy, in the Preface to *Caravan*, points out that a writer who decides to write pot-boilers for a few years because he believes that they will give him the income he needs in order to write the things he wants, is likely to come to nothing. The man who stays at home in order to make the money with which to travel is in the same condition. He will go through the motions, no doubt. He may see the Taj Mahal and the Golden Gate, Rio de Janeiro and the Alhambra, but it will be too late for him to travel in the only way that matters—because of necessity. If you haven't *got* to travel, you may as well stay at home.

By 'necessity' I do not mean under orders as soldiers are on troopships. I mean the inner necessity which drives a man to travel though it may be against his more facile inclinations, against discretion, against the will of others; to travel when he cannot afford it, when he is not fit for it, when it means sacrifice and insecurity. I have never had much patience with young people who pass their lives in day-to-day monotony, only pausing to sigh and bemoan their necessity to remain where they are. 'If only I could break away, go abroad, do something else . . .' they say, and the passing years see them bound more tightly to the wheel. If they really wanted to break away they could do so.

That is the kind of travel I have in mind, the kind of travel that is done when one can't afford to travel at all, when one is taking a risk of being stranded somewhere. I don't mean necessarily emigrating. It may be the traveller's intention to return when some of his curiosity has been satisfied, when his urge to see other countries and people has been appeased. But 'travel for its own sake', pleasure-cruising or mere globetrotting are no more than the physical motions of travel. I have myself made many journeys for which I was not equipped or which I could not afford. I remember once travelling from London to Barcelona third-class on

slow trains, sitting on wooden benches for eight hours at a
time, watching the consumption of curious provender by
my fellow travellers and finally waking from my own sleep
to find an unconscious head on each of my shoulders and an
atmosphere of garlic and black tobacco which was so potent
as to seem almost gaseous. That journey cost £8, I believe,
and I undertook it with no more than £20 in the world—
and only that much because I had sold my books to raise it.
Yet as we came into Barcelona at night, and for the first
time I saw the Ramblas, that tree-lined walk which is as
populous and well-lit at four in the morning as at four in the
afternoon, I would not have changed my place with that of
any Englishman driving up to the Barcelona Ritz in a taxi
which had brought him from the airport.

As for being 'stranded'—that bogy of the half-hearted
adventurer—it is rare indeed, no more probable than that
one will be stranded in Edinburgh or Truro. And even if it
comes to pass, one doesn't after all starve to death or take
to crime or become a beachcomber, unless one is already a
potential suicide or criminal or sponger. One comes through
this as through everything else by the will to survive it and
the intelligence necessary to defeat the forces against one.
The experience fell to me once when I was too young immediately to find the way out of it. And even for that,
unpleasant though it was, I am not unthankful, for I lost
nothing but a pound or two in weight and a few rather
silly illusions.

I was nineteen at the time and in Buenos Aires. The
combination of circumstances which caused the situation
is of no importance. I found myself penniless, homeless,
hungry one evening and with no means of support, visible
or invisible. I remained thus for three days until I was
relieved in a way which also need not be specified.

Three days does not sound a long time. When I read the
stories of splendid adventurers who go for weeks through a
desert, tropical or Arctic, without proper supplies, I am
bound to confess that three days of destitution in a hot city
sounds a meagre sort of privation. But then it seemed a

month, a year—it had no limit in time. Sometimes during those seventy-two hours, I felt that I never should escape, that I should die there of starvation, or fever, or mere misery.

I walked, because I have always found it impossible to stand still in a street. The movement of the people about me draws me with it, however tired I am. I walked, I think, through almost every street of the city, out to Avellaneda, to the Recoleta, to Liniers. And then back again, quite pointlessly. During nearly all that time I was hungry and for much of it was literally starving. The very use of that word sounds whining, as though even from this distance I were trying to arouse sympathy. Nothing of the sort. I use it because it conveys the simple truth—I was in a state of semi-starvation.

There seem, now, perhaps, to be a hundred and one things that I could have done. I could have written or cabled to my father. But how would I pay for the cable or even the stamp? And even if I could have done that, there would have been a delay of weeks in the case of a letter, and days in that of a cable, where it was always *now* that I wanted money and food, now, in that very minute. That, I think, is what accounts for the making of beachcombers. They need so much at that very minute that they cannot be expected to think of the future. They cannot even think far enough ahead to look for work. They want food, a drink, tobacco, *now*. And they will do anything to obtain it.

That was how I felt. I would, I assured myself, do anything to obtain it. And yet, when I thought of something to do, my nerve seemed to fail, and I slouched away. Quite early in the long agony, on the first morning, after a night on a bench in a plaza, I went to two different Englishmen I knew for help. To one of them I had actually lent money in the past. Both refused it. I do not blame them for that. There were far too many English beachcombers clinging to the charity of the British colony for them to be easily touched. And I suppose that they could scarcely be blamed for disbelieving my story. Or perhaps they thought I should ask for more, either now or in the future, and that it was best to make it clear from the first that they were not disposed to be generous. At all events they refused, and that broke my nerve, I think. So I turned to the charity of the streets.

In that, I suppose, as such things go, I was as lucky as most, for I was unable actually to ask for anything. Once again, I state a simple fact. Hunger makes one mad. I would walk along knowing that if I was certain to escape all consequence of the act, I would have murdered the next passerby for money with which to buy food. Only the law, and fear of its powers and penalties, restrained me from theft. For hunger wipes out, with an ease which is surprising to a civilized person, most kinds of moral or personal scruple. It turns one into a mere feline scavenger, prowling round for food. And yet, although it did that for me, although I had no scruple whatever left in me, I could not, however hard I tried, enunciate the words necessary for begging.

Fortunately, however, the sort of person who would be responsive to them does not always need to be asked. A bartender—or he may have been the proprietor—of a small café in Leandro Alem, whom I had asked for a glass of water, gave me a packet of sandwiches made the day before. I could always ask for water, because it cost nothing. What absurdities our training and character teach us. Famished, parched, quite blind and senseless with despair, I distinguished between asking for water and asking for bread, because anyone, even an affluent and well-fed person, might ask for water, and only a beggar would ask for bread. Another time, I think it was during the third day when I had stubble on my chin and my clothes were dirty, I awoke from a sleep on a plaza bench to find a large piece of garlic-scented sausage and a hunk of bread beside me. So that I was not perhaps in danger, in those seventy-two hours, of death from starvation.

And all the time—and I would like you not to laugh—all the time there was something in me which said that this was life, this was experience, this was what I had come to South America to feel. What insight I was gaining! What enlightenment! If ever I should escape from this torrid inferno, I should look back on these days as some of the most valuable in my life. For wasn't I going to be a writer? And did not writers proverbially learn from such suffering as this?

I do not know quite what I learnt from it, still less what I gained. I learnt that a hungry man is nothing but a living desire, that all thought, belief, determination, is wholly obliterated by that desire, that he will do anything to satisfy it, and that in all judgments on the actions of hungry men, we should take this into account. And I learnt the truth of yet another truism—that human beings are not really ill-disposed or ungenerous, as one might sometimes suppose, but ready enough to help one another when they see the need. As for gain—perhaps a little understanding and tolerance, perhaps a sharpening of that part of my imagination which is concerned with the misfortunes of others. But I cannot pretend, even now, when the agony and misery of it is a memory, that it was in any sense worthwhile.

Yet in those three days I became, in a very special sense, a *porteño*, a citizen of Buenos Aires. Perhaps there is some truth in the old idea that there is an underside to every great city, seen only by the outcast. Perhaps hunger and wretchedness give a certain clarity to one's vision of streets and people. I do not know. But I do believe that I learnt something about Buenos Aires in that time which I could have learnt in no other way. I woke stiff-jointed and stale from a few hours' sleep, and saw morning come up from the Plate, and the earliest workers pass. I wanted a bath more than anything, I believe, more even than hot coffee and rolls. Three days without a change of clothes in that heat, without a shave, and with a chance only for a sur- reptitious wash of face and hands now and again, makes one loathe oneself. And time behaved eccentrically. There would be an afternoon which would seem interminable, for I would pass clocks several times on my walks and find them apparently unmoved. And another day, or a morning would go by over my head in an hour as it seemed, and I would see that it was noon, and know that although I had travelled that much from the last food I had eaten, I was no nearer to any more.

There was another odd sensation—that of detachment from the rest of the populace. Before, though I might have had no money at the time, I was one with the passing crowd. Now I was isolated. I imagined myself, perhaps, more conspicuously shabby than I was, since I felt so miserably unclean. If I walked along a pavement I felt the passers-by to be of one species, myself of another. Anyone who has gone through a similar experience will understand this, I think. Destitution makes one feel as a leper must have felt in Palestine. One imagines a drawing away of skirts, a stepping off the pavement by a child, a look from another man, to be significant.

Three days—it was soon over, and soon forgotten, and it has never seemed quite real. A part of the time—the second evening in particular—I passed in a state which cannot have been far from delirium, for I remember repeating to myself, and once or twice aloud, some crazy phrase or other, and I remember making foolish resolves which I never started to carry out. And I remember a little policeman in the Plaza Congreso watching me for a long time, as though he were debating the advisability of arresting me. And since I knew of no offence I had committed I supposed then and thereafter that I must have said or done something to rouse his suspicion, without being aware of it.

When I had returned to normal life, the whole thing soon became a short chapter, a small piece stitched on to the coloured patchwork of the past. In retrospect it certainly does nothing to lessen my belief that if one wants to travel, one should not wait till one can do so in comfort. Counted against the wonders of that early voyage to South America it is less than nothing. To have seen the River Plate, that vast sweet-water sea which changes colour with the clouds above it, to know the beauty of the pampas, those rich levels stretching from the Andes to the coast, a separate element, it seems, neither land nor ocean but partaking of the characteristics of each; to have seen the jewelled white city of Rio de Janeiro under its bright emerald hills with islands sporting like porpoises in the deep blue water of its bay; to have lived among the most vigorous and virile people of modern times—all these seem important, not the fact that my improvidence once brought me to despair.

And so it was always with me. I was prepared at any time to sell all I had and mortgage what I should earn in order to see more of the world. When, just before the last war, it was the fashion to write books about the European situation which either predicted the forthcoming horrors or lulled their readers into seeing Hitler and Mussolini as jolly, friendly fellows who wouldn't hurt a fly, and certainly not a British one, I hit on the notion of interviewing not the dictators and the publicized men of fate, but the man in the street in Europe. I decided to travel through as many countries as possible spending my time in café-talk and street-talk, trying to understand how the ordinary citizen felt about things. This time a publisher was prepared to support the idea, and I determined to set out in winter when Europe would be for the most part free of tourists. I bought an old Morris sixteen-seater bus which had done twelve years' service on the Welsh roads, and converted it into a living-wagon with bunks and a stove since my publisher's confidence in the scheme did not extend to the cost of hotels. With two circus-artists, brothers, who had spent their lives in such living-wagons and were infinitely resourceful and reliable, I set out to see life from the road. Through Belgium, right across Germany we went without let or hindrance, though it was the winter of 1937–8. To Prague and down to Vienna, fighting our way through the snow without even a skid-chain, and then to the graceful city of Budapest and across a still almost mediaeval Hungary into Yugoslavia.

It was the gayest journey I have ever made. We had prepared for it in less than two weeks, which included the time necessary for converting the wagon. We had not nearly enough money, but with rum at a shilling a bottle and milk almost for the asking, we could sip our hot grog over our stove at night while the snow fell, and eat as much country produce as we wanted. We demanded no more. When we had crossed the North of Italy and reached the Riviera and found ourselves in a new world of English visitors, crowded casinos and expensive sunshine, we felt no more ill-at-ease than we had in the market squares where our wagon had stood in Eastern Europe, and we pulled in beside the promenade at Mentone without embarrassment. And so home after three months' travelling through ten countries. I know no better way of seeing the world.

Another way of moving about England without struggling for the mediocre comfort of hotels, I discovered in the early months of the war when I bought a horse-drawn caravan and with Ted Scamp as my sole companion lived on the road and among other gypsies. Our journey was not a long one in distance, though we were nearly two months on the road, staying several days in some places and some weeks at Goudhurst because of a fall of snow. It was not a grand trek across England, with nights spent in general encampments or days of journeying as one of a string of wagons. It was long enough to give me the sense of the thing, the feeling of being one of a vagrant people, to see the suspicion in men's faces, and once to know the majestic stupidity of the Law. And it was varied as all good travelling must be, taking us through two counties and most kinds of winter and early spring weather, and bringing us into contact with some nicely contrasted people. But it did not carry us through the summer or to the Welsh mountains. It was a dawdling pleasant journey through parts of Kent and Sussex which ended as unexpectedly as it had begun. It was not made without difficulties, for the house-dweller and the Law have little sympathy for the *romani's* need to pull in by a roadside, and once, at least, this was evident. We were sitting by the warm stove of our *vardo* on a cold night of heavy mist when there was a sudden very noisy banging on the door. It seemed that Ted had been expecting this, for he signed me not to move, went out, and shut the door behind him.

'Can't stop here,' I heard.

'Well what d'you expect us to do? Got no lights.'

'Can't help that. Can't stop here.'

'You expect us to go on and then pinch us for being on the road without any lights, then?'

There was a brief silence. I found this dialogue out of the darkness to have a certain dramatic quality.

'Where's your horse?' asked the strange voice, clearly a policeman's.

'Down the road,' said Ted instantly, but vaguely.

'Well, you can't stop here.'

The policeman did not seem to be much of a conversationalist.

'Well, we can't move,' said Ted, who was growing tautological, too.

'Been up round that farm, haven't you?'

'So that's who's sent you along, is it? I thought so. All I asked him was if we could put the horse in his paddock. Offered to pay him, 'n' everything.'

'Anyway, you can't stop on the side of the road like this. *You* know that, very well.'

'You tell me what else I'm to do. Drive on tonight in this mist without any lights?'

'That's nothing to do with it. You'll have to move from here. Why didn't you get in somewhere while it was still light?'

'How was we to know there was mist coming? We're not doing any harm, are we?'

'You know you're not allowed to pull in on the verge like that. And I'd like to know where your horse is. How many is there of you?'

'Two,' said Ted.

'Well, I've warned you. I'll be back again presently and if you've not gone, you know what'll happen.'

Ted came back and settled down again by the fire.

'Shan't see him again,' he remarked, and set about the preparation of rum and hot milk.

'How do you know, Ted?'

'If he could of done anything, he'd of done it then. He just wanted to save his face. That farmer must have telephoned down to him. But what *could* he do? He daren't put us on the road without lights. You don't want to take any notice of that. That's nothing. We shall always be getting the *mushgros* round about something or other. They can't see a *vardo* without having a go at it.'

That was the best hour of each day, when the journey, such as it was, had been accomplished, the horse unharnessed and disposed of for the night, the steps brought from the back of the wagon and set in place, the fire blazing up and the lamp lit. Then we would stretch our limbs as best we might and sit smoking silently while the kettle boiled for tea.

And how we ate! The fresh air, the day's exercise, the quick roadside lunch, gave us, at five or six o'clock, horses' appetites. But although Ted ate a great deal, he had fastidious table manners and never set a meal on the table unless there was a decently clean cloth on it and polished crockery and cutlery. He told me once that his blessed old *daia* had taught them, not without a cuff or two, to eat carefully, even if the plates were on their knees out of doors. But we never hurried to clear away or wash up the tea-things, for it was over these that we talked, and in exchange for Ted's inexhaustible stock of gypsy stories I would try to answer his sometimes bewildering questions about aspects of *gorgio*, and particularly of London, life with which he was unfamiliar. That is the sort of travelling for me, unmapped, unpremeditated, comfortable in the most real sense but not without hardships and surprises. Above all showing the land one knew, the familiar people, from an angle entirely new. Viewed from the half-door of a caravan, England is a strange country.

Even in the Army during the war I found that the will to see more of other countries could overcome many of the more obvious limitations imposed by discipline. Training in Combined Operations took us to Scapa Flow, and a story told by a marine that an unauthorized photograph had been taken of our activities ashore got me permission to spend a few nights in the Orkneys to investigate. And an unexpected last embarkation leave, after family farewells had been said, took me to the Isle of Barra to stay with Compton Mackenzie and see something of the astonishing Hebrides, the islands which have never changed their faith. When our convoy finally left Gourock to make its way to South Africa, so that we lay in Freetown harbour for a night, on some pretext connected with the mail I got myself sent ashore and can still smell that crawling city.

In Madagascar when we had made our landings, it took more ingenuity to gain freedom of movement, but one way or another I managed to see most of the island, from the little groups of huts which the timid Malagache calls villages to the fantastic hilltop city of Tananarive, where the castle of the last native ruler is still filled with her barbaric jewellery and baroque furniture, and where outer walls have been built to enclose the wooden framework of the original palace, since the Queen could not bear to destroy her original wood walls, though she had been told that her dignity demanded stonework.

In South Africa, where we went to recuperate from the feverish maladies of Madagascar, it was a piece of luck rather than any action on my part, which enabled me to go up into Zululand. A bout of malaria took me to hospital in Pietermaritzburg and I came out to find that my unit had left for India and that I had two months to pass in Durban before I could rejoin it. Permission to enter the Zulu reserves was granted and I found myself squatting beside the rich old chief M'tubatuba, who presented me some examples of Zulu craftsmanship which are my proud possession to this day. Christmas I spent with an old French priest at one of the loneliest missions in Africa. He had been sent to the place twenty years ago, and persuading the Zulus to carry the stones on their heads from ten miles away, he had built his own church and home and school. It seemed romantic to me, I remember, that the only way of reaching the mission was on horseback and that I rode for a day across the fresh undulating hills to find the old priest, white-bearded and tall like an ancient prophet, waiting to welcome me.

The will to travel, which may after all be no more than curiosity, becomes a habit, and a few days at Mombasa during our Madagascar operations were sufficient to send me into the remoter parts of that curious city—the Jewish and the Arab quarters. I remember a little Arab general shop where I would sit during the afternoon, noting down words of Arabic, beginning to stutter my first phrases and drinking coffee with the shopkeeper, hot, scented coffee bought from an itinerant vendor.

Then, at last, India. I think now that all the countries I had seen before I went ashore at Bombay might be considered as no more than a preparation for this, as though the thirty-four of them had existed only for me as experiences sufficient to give me a sense of proportion with which to understand 'enchanted Hind'.

I saw much of it, and no man can say more than that, for India is a continent rather than a country, and one could spend a lifetime learning to understand a little of one of its areas. Bombay first, a city of great contrasts and glaring colours and such multitudes upon multitudes of inhabitants that never anywhere in its streets, day or night, could one count less than a hundred people in sight and sometimes a thousand or more. That, indeed, was my first impression of India—the density of its population.

South to Belgaum, north to Dehra Dun whence one could go up to Missourhi and see the eternal snows, west to Karachi, east to Calcutta—there was no considerable area which I did not manage to visit. And when I found myself a Field Security officer with an area the size of England and Wales to explore without interference, driving a Cadillac station-wagon with a couple of sepoys as my companions, I could have asked for no more. From the borders of Mysore to Ahmednagar, from the Konkoni coast to the frontier of

Hyderabad, I went, making what I deemed it necessary to call 'security tours' and learning every day a little more of the most interesting land of the modern world.

To see yet another country within a country I persuaded Southern Army Headquarters that good purpose would be served if they allowed me to go on leave to Goa. No larger than a small English county, this then Portuguese possession was strangely different from what was then British India, for the tradition of the early settler, sternly Catholic and richly civilized, persisted almost unchanged. There is another almost deserted city here, the baroque shell of Old Goa, once the greatest city of the East, now a few ruined houses and some vast churches, in one of which lies the embalmed body of St Francis Xavier. The Goanese Indians live in a happy Occidental way and cargoes of good wine were still arriving in the port. I was lucky to have that experience, for it was a closed country to the British throughout the war. There were interned German seamen and a few Italians who had escaped from prison camps in India to give it the air of a neutral country, though the frontier was a rather haphazard affair a few miles away.

Later, established once more as a Field Security officer at Delhi with all the Central States to drive through, the rose-red city of Bikaner in the heart of its desert or the great temples of Khajrao standing in solitude beyond the tourist's ken, but certainly making one of the marvels of the world, even my lust for more to see and hear and explore was almost sated.

So as a penniless writer, as a journalist with no expense sheet, as a soldier, I managed to travel a fair proportion of the world's surface, but never in order to escape an English winter or to feel sunshine in February. I went because I could not stay still, because whatever sacrifice was necessary had to be made, because I wanted more than anything to see other lands. And I know now that it was the best way. Such tame travel as I have done since the war has proved it to me. Taking a car across to Denmark and motoring through Sweden and Norway is a pleasant enough way of spending a month, but it is no more. Travelling on a ship which calls at ten Spanish ports so that one has a day or two ashore in Bilbao, Seville, Barcelona and so on, makes an agreeable summer holiday but is not travel as I understand it. Or going, as I did one summer, to work for a month in that strange area of pine-trees and nightingales which runs inland from the coast for a hundred miles between Bordeaux and Biarritz may be an excellent way to work and escape the miseries of English postwar diet, but who could call it travelling? No, travel is more than an impulse or an urge, it is a prime necessity, and for those of us who feel it, there can be no escape. It is a comforting thought that however it may be facilitated and accelerated, there must always be enough of the world's surface to last a human lifetime.

So it can be understood that when young David returned a fortnight or so after his departure, I was pleased that he called on me an hour or two after he had docked at Southampton and as soon as he reached Bournemouth.

He needed no questioning. 'I had about thirty quid when I left Bournemouth,' he said. 'I thought that would be enough to get me to Sweden, specially as I meant to hitch most of the way. I was quite cheery when I set off and had no difficulty hitching a lift to Brighton, which was on my way—round the coast towards Dover. I'd never been in that part of the world—yours, isn't it?—and I liked the look of Brighton. I went into a pub there and got into conversation with the barmaid—went on talking till closing time.'

It was useless to try to follow his timing and I did not know whether he had arrived in Brighton on the first or second day. But I gathered that when he left the bar a storm was raging which was one of the worst for thirty years. Force 9 to 11 winds, he learned afterwards, and driving rain. He had to find somewhere to sleep and went into a block of flats where a cupboard under the stairs where brooms were kept was all he could find for sleeping quarters. But next morning he got a good lift to Hastings—a man who was out early in the morning, 'the kind that keeps complaining of his wife'—'a bit of a bore but friendly enough and took me right into the town'. David hadn't eaten that morning and went into a café and paid for a hot drink and food. He was taken on to Rye (with which 'pretty little town' he said he was 'impressed', as well he might have been) and from there a soldier returning to Germany from leave with an old car of his own gave him a lift to Dover. The day was bright and clear after the storm and he liked Dover, where he spent most of the day, again talking to a barmaid. He paid his passage to Ostend; when he had made the crossing, he discovered that of his £30, only a fiver remained. He seemed mightily puzzled about this but did not try to explain it by blaming anyone else. 'It had just happened,' he said, but at least he would get as far as Ostend.

I liked this attitude. Never in the course of my own wanderings could I have accepted with Bhuddistic detachment the loss or theft of nearly all the money I had. David only remarked that he had slept in the Ostend terminus when he reached it for what remained of the night, and went on to tell me how he had made his way to Antwerp, and being given a lift through Bruges (of happy memories to me) and Ghent, saw little of either.

He was lucky then. A car already crowded with the members of a large Belgian family, father, mother, sons and daughters, made room for him somehow and took him right into the city of Antwerp to find the Labour Exchange. They had to go the last of the way on foot, and David liked the picture of himself leading this formidable troop to the doors of the building where they bid him goodbye and good luck and marched away.

He never seemed altogether certain whether the building was that of Labour Exchange, Salvation Army Hostel, Sailors' Rest or Mission to Seamen, though he stayed there for two weeks and was given work to pay his board, humping new tyres. He did not mind this, having a muscular and indefatigable frame, but he could find no chance of getting a ship from that port, and staying there did not bring him much nearer to his goal. When he was paid for his first week's work, he settled with the Sailors' Rest and in accordance with the custom of his calling, went out and got drunk at a disco. On his way home through the narrow back streets, he was mugged, and although he reached the Sailors' Rest without greater damage, he woke up to find he had been cleaned out—not only of paper money but the few pieces of nickel he had in his pockets.

At this point I became more interested in the story, for I also, at less than his age, had found myself quite penniless in the unsympathetic city of Buenos Aires, and I wanted to know how David would treat the matter. I was not surprised to hear that he fell in with another seaman in like straits, and for a time they shared their misfortunes. The seaman was a Hungarian refugee who had been through many of the troubles of his country and blamed most of them on Russians, for whom he felt a white-hot hatred which inspired all his talk of the past. David never knew his name and made no enquiries about his story; together they simply made their situation a little lighter, or at least more bearable than it would have been singly.

Each of them, after several days of hunger, realized that he had some family connection to which he could appeal, and each of them did this. David wrote to his father in the North of England, the Hungarian to his sister in France. David's father responded with some money and good-natured amusement (an 'I might have known' sort of jibe). The Hungarian's sister did not reply, but his faith in her was such that they spent a week waiting for the result that they believed was on its way before they eventually gave up hope.

Their time was up at the Seamen's Rest and/or Labour Exchange, and for several days after David's father's money had run out they subsisted on scrounging foodstuffs, usually vegetables and fruit. David gave me a vivid description of eating a carrot and told me of the joy which a pocketed ripe pear had meant. They slept in the cellar of a block of flats until they were evicted, and thereafter shared the shelter of some scaffolding with a hopeless alcoholic—methylated spirits probably.

At last, realizing forcefully that something had to be done, they decided to move by some means or other to Paris, where the Hungarian thought they could obtain work and at least a place to eat and sleep. So they jumped trains.

Now according to the makers of American films this, in their country, is a simple matter of boarding a wagon of a goods train and sleeping snugly while it crosses the continent. I have no knowledge of the truth or otherwise of this picture, never having jumped a train in America, but I could readily believe that the process is vastly more difficult in Europe. However, neither of the two young men was naive or totally inexperienced, and by elaborate wiles in concealment and innocent answering ('My friend has the tickets') and a trick of actually sitting on the seat of the loo with trousers down to embarrass the most persistent of ticket-collectors, they managed to cross the frontier before the Hungarian was nicked and removed from the train. The last David saw of him was being led cheerfully away by a couple of *flics*, while David continued his journey to Paris unsuspected.

He had never been to Paris and knew no one there. Again he slept in a cupboard under the stairs of a block of flats somewhere (he thinks) on the South Bank. He found a bottle of milk that morning which kept him alive through the day, but to steal it, he says, was as difficult as stealing something of great value, a fact few people realize, especially since it seems more shameful. 'I shouldn't mind being pinched for knocking off a piece of jewellery,' David says, 'but I'd feel pretty cheap being charged as a milk-bottle bandit.' I could understand this paradoxical logic.

But he did not have to suffer that humiliation, for when he was arrested, as he was next day, it was not for stealing milk but for being suspected of taking *kif*. He had stopped on the pavement to roll a cigarette, having long since given up buying cigarettes by the packet, when a purposeful policeman took him to the nearest police-station. Here he was stripped and thoroughly searched for marihuana. When nothing was found on him, he was told curtly to dress and get out, without a smile or word of apology, and although afterwards he met and made friends with a black policeman from Guadeloupe who gave him cigarettes and a beer, this could not smooth out his resentment against those in the police station.

Paris was the end of the road for David, and he related the events of his return journey with some confusion. There was the same vigilance and deception to avoid the ticket-collector, this time without a partner, but he reached Le Havre without notable incident. Here he appears to have gone by road towards Calais, for he remembers being 'out in the country' in darkness without a dwelling or a human being in sight. He thinks he trudged on for nearly an hour until one solitary light in a window told him he was not quite alone in the world and he made for it.

I felt for him and shared his sense of relief and gratitude at finding a large hospitable family who were sitting up waiting for the arrival of their married daughter from Paris. Had these people, I wondered, some experience of lost British soldiers in wartime? They invited David in, fed him and gave him wine, arranged a bed for him and offered him a bath, which was what he wanted above all things. He might have been the prodigal son, he says, when they asked him to stay on if he wanted, and drove him to Calais with his pockets packed with provisions and cigarettes. I confess I wondered at first whether this bounteous reception had not been an illusion imagined by David in his state of semi-starvation and fatigue, but he assured me several days after the event that it was nothing of the sort, and he insisted that in return for any use his story had been to me I should write of his gratitude to that family so that he can send them a copy of the book. This at once convinced me and I hope I have expressed what he wanted.

Well, that was three weeks ago and I have not seen David since. But I am not surprised. Once a young man has learned to travel by whatever means and with whatever (or no) object, he will not remain long at home, and I have no doubt that sooner or later he will knock at my door with another story to tell which will remind me, as this one does, of my own irresponsible itineraries.

He made few comments on his exploits, seeming to think that his task was to narrate, not to criticize. His Hungarian friend was, he said, 'brave but devious like most stateless people he had met'. He was amused that after his mischievous but unpunished adventures, and after passing through the British Customs unmolested, he was in trouble with the highway police for walking on a motorway to reach Bournemouth. All he had got from a thorough investigation of telephone boxes abroad was one franc, and all he had learned of any practical value in Paris was that the Gare du Nord closed its waiting-rooms at eleven o'clock. Finally, that four of the most generous passers-by he had met were some students carrying a banner whose purport he never knew. 'Might have been Communists or Catholics —who the hell cares? They bought me a drink and a packet of Gauloises.' He said little about his wife and little son, seeming to think that they formed no part of a story told to a writer for his use or pleasure. To me it gave both.

Nine

A Group of Noble Dames

After recounting these adventures of a young friend I think it is a suitable point in this book to answer one accusation against it—namely that it is misogynic. A false inference from this—if it were true—would be that the writer has the bias of a homosexual, a suggestion belied by the fact that many, perhaps most, homosexuals adore women and seek to copy them, are mother-lovers to an almost Oedipian degree and prefer the conversation and company of women to those of their own sex.

'You,' intelligent accusers have said more than once, 'you obviously loved your father, but scarcely mention your mother. You rarely talk of girls and your male friends are manifold.'

I deny the implication. My mother, however lovable, as indeed she was to me, was a more conventional person and from a far more conventional family than my father, and her well-meaning attempts in my boyhood to check my own eccentricities (which my father took for granted) often led her into acts of inquisitive invasion of my most sacred privacy. In the earlier years she had a formidable rival in my childish love in the person of Ninna, the nurse whose imaginative (though modest) inventiveness gave me so much happiness till she left us to emigrate to Canada, leaving me to hear the news of her departure while I was away at my preparatory school, where I secretly cried myself to sleep under the bedclothes. She was killed in a traffic accident in London, Ontario, during the late war, and that news reached me while I was serving in India, and moved me almost as deeply. I admired my mother as a pianist and for her qualities as a matriarch in her last years, and I loved her in the somewhat conventional way of a son to whom it had never occurred *not* to do so, but I readily admit that I was wholly devoted to my father as a parent of understanding and encouragement. I could laugh with my brother Laurie at my father's faults and oddities: to laugh at my mother would have been too painful for both of us.

But there were other women of whom I was sensitively conscious in my earliest years. My godmother, Bella Whitehead, for instance. She was the only truly sophisticated and elegant woman—as it seemed to me—who enlightened my boyhood. She lived in a large comfortable flat with her sister in Hampstead, from which she went to first nights and told me of them when I went to see her. She was on visiting terms with a number of people of distinction and discussed books with me when I had reached the age of opinions. She first came to stay with us at Little Sunte when I was no more than three ('three years old and a man', I used to quote proudly when I was asked) and the impression of a shimmering dress, a scent and a pleasant-speaking voice remained with me until a few years before her death, when I went to see her in the private hotel in Malvern to which she had retired.

Who dares talk of misogyny who has read my account of Miss Wain, the heavenly governess, in *The Gardens of Camelot*? Or who would do so who remembers Annie Dickson described in the same book? Then there was the 'grown-up girl' at the postponed garden party for the Coronation of George V with whom I fell in love at eight years old in 1911.

There were moreover two lovable aunts, one a sister of my mother, the other of my father, who had been kept at their respective family homes in the manner of those days to look after their ageing parents. I hope I did justice to 'Aunt Fo-Fo' in the earlier books of this series and her addiction to the various arts and crafts of her time. It was typical of her courage and ingenuity when at seventy-eight she became blind, she learned to use Braille quite faultlessly for the last nine years of her life, but I only realized her charm during the 1920s when we used to meet in Warrior Square, Hastings. The other beloved aunt was Auntie Renie whose familiar name would have shocked her father 'the Emperor', who by a philological fancy had called his daughters by Greek names (Agatha, Xenia and Eirene) and his sons by Anglo-Saxon ones, Selwyn, Herbert and Hubert. She was so different from her sister-in-law that she might have belonged to another species. Brought up under the tyranny of the Emperor, her only escape in childhood, like the Brontës' was in story-telling, a faculty she retained along with her colourless, matronly clothes and her pince-nez glasses to her old age. In my childhood I remember her stories about a character called Old Noodlums and how he was tricked out of his pocket-money and overcoat by a stranger who persuaded him to go into a shop while he disappeared. Thrilling stuff it was when I was five years old and loved any story that was told with spirit. I saw Auntie Renie last just after the Second World War when she shared a cottage with Aunt Xenia, lent to them by the Croft family near the home of Uncle Septimus and my godfather Philip Croft at Ware in Hertfordshire. She had no more stories for me then, but she was still the lovable and loving Victorian aunt whom I remembered from childhood. Of her, and of many other women in my life whom I have loved or respected, made friends or laughed with, who have been companions in my childhood, my teens, my maturity and now old age, I shall write now, and so, I hope, give the lie to those who have called me antagonistic to women, or more justly shy of them. I am antagonistic to the preposterous absurdities which an ignorant Government has tried to introduce under the Sex Discrimination Act, but to women themselves whom I have loved too much to marry, to the lovely girls and sympathetic matrons I have known throughout life, I have felt no antipathy at all, and here, in the last book of this series, which is in some senses a summing-up, is the time to show it.

My sister Olive, whom I have described affectionately in *The Ghost of June*, was the one girl among five brothers, and as she preferred to be treated as one of these, she never had for me the aura and mystery of femininity. We two were together a good deal in childhood and are now the only two remaining of our family, but Olive still rides horseback and I still write, so I suppose we are fortunate to have outlived our brothers.

In my teens I certainly had a shyness of girls of similar age, though I remember sentimental and not very physical affairs with two of them with whom I corresponded until I found that my letters were being shown to impress other girls in school. One of them was Kitty Foote whom I not only adored but from whom I learned much of the ways and tastes of schoolgirls. She had read a popular novel by Gene Stratton Porter and wanted me to sign my letters by the name of its title 'Freckles'. I might have managed this but Kitty had an elder brother at Tonbridge who used his authority as a 'day-boy's house-prae' (an anomalous title as any Tonbridgian can see) in order to curry favour with a genuine school praepostor who accused me of bullying a boy older and more powerful than myself. This I imagine ended my tentative approaches to his sister, and Kitty and I never met again.

Then there was the admirable Marjorie Kellett-Smith in Eastbourne whom I—greatly daring—invited to tea in Bobby's Café where a three-man orchestra played selections from a list provided to patrons with their tea. I thought Marjorie was wonderful, and to show my enthusiasm I quote from *The Drums of Morning*:

'When we went back to our respective schools Marjorie and I exchanged letters, but that may have been to show off again.

'Twenty years later in Cheltenham I met an aged Doctor Kellett-Smith and asked him if he had a daughter called Marjorie. Yes, she was happily married and so on; why did I ask? Because years ago, as a boy of sixteen, I said,

I had admired her and never dared to show it. I had seen her often, taken her to a café for tea and thought she was the nicest girl in Eastbourne if not in the world, though I had never told her so. The old doctor seemed to take this as a personal slight.

' "You weren't the only one who admired her, not by a a long way," he said. "Don't get *that* idea into your head. If you think you were the only pebble on the beach you're very much mistaken."

' "No. Of course. I only . . ."

' "Knew her when we lived in Eastbourne, did you? I daresay. Knew a lot of people there. But you're making a mistake if you think no one else ran after her as a girl. I don't remember you or anything about you, but I can assure you my daughter had all the admirers *she* wanted. And more. So don't make any mistake about that."

'I gave it up. But across the years I salute her who showed no boredom with my egotistical and confused character, who let me show her to my schoolfriend as "a girl I know", who went with me to that dingy little den the Old Town Cinema and above all who answered my letters from school so that I too, among the Midlanders and Northerners with their girls, their fiancées, their "birds", could show that I knew someone who signed herself "yours affectionately" (no more) "Marjorie". '

To demonstrate that I was not unaware of physical beauty in girls I must recall a Hastings doctor's daughter named Monica Ballingall. I think even now, after studying human physiognomies of many races, she was a singularly beautiful young woman, but my damnable shyness with girls, perhaps due to my only sister's easy boyishness, prevented me from hinting of that even when I went with her to hear the election results of 1921 in which our candidate Lord Eustace Percy was pronounced triumphant. Oh yes, Monica Ballingall was lovely, but perhaps no one could have been so notably so, with her peach-dark Italianate skin and musing eyes, as idealization has made her seem in recollection to me for the last half-century.

Yet another young beauty of a very different appearance and disposition was Hilda Green, the Scandinavian-blonde daughter of a Nonconformist Minister in St Leonards. I thought her petulant and spoilt, and she had a crowd of hearty and jocose brothers, but I had rather unwillingly to admit that she was pretty. I do not quite remember the details but I know our friendship ended in angry reproofs from her mother and a report to my "Auntie Annie" with whom I was staying that I was *not* a nice boy to know.

This kind of categorization of the girls I knew has its absurdity, but having begun it, I will not cause annoyance to any of them who may chance to be alive and who see these pages, either by omitting them altogether or by pretending to a greater intimacy than in fact I achieved. I have spoken of those I admired in childhood, but more interesting perhaps are those who were more or less contemporaries of mine and whom I knew in my later teens and early twenties. For instance, the artist Evelyn Dunbar whose obituary I noted a year or two back, who was my friend in the days I had a bookshop in Rochester and who not only began painting a portrait of me but desgined the wrappers of my first two novels. She was the wayward daughter of a successful furniture remover and I fondly remember going to dances with her in a miniature palais at which the tunes of the early thirties were played by an unforgettable band.

Another artist who achieved distinction was Pearl Binder whom I met among young painters and writers in London. She did some brilliant black and white drawings to illustrate quatrains of mine, and I remember long café conversations with her which led of course nowhere, though I sincerely admired her and her work. A more real, perhaps I can say more passionate, relationship was with a certain young woman called Y who lived a bus-ride away from the tiny cottage I rented at Wrotham, as described in *The Purple Streak*. She used to jump off the Maidstone and District bus as it slowed down before the crossroads and arrive at my cottage unannounced. She always brought something for me which was welcome in that penurious time—a cake or a box of biscuits which she had made—and when tea was drunk and I had eaten some of her offerings, she would pull off her clothes and lie on the bed like Goya's famous nude, as restless as one feels was the original. She was a lovely girl.

Another friend of that period—or rather earlier—was one of a clever family, children of a Scottish employee of McAlpines. Her name when I knew her was Grace Nesbitt but afterwards she married an actor called Wyndham Goldie and became a leading light of broadcasting. Then I was grateful to her for her good advice about my early novels and her tactful discouragement of ideas which were probably inadvisable, to say the least of it.

Best and most intelligent of all among the young women I had as friends in that awkward period between my teens and my later twenties was a parson's daughter called Mollie Schwaby. When I knew her first it was as the sub-editor of a curious periodical called *The Reader* which was edited by G. B. Harrison. Mollie was a splendid talkative girl who disliked my friends almost as much as I did hers, and was greatly amused when during a walk from Bromley I told her that I had been trying to ask her to marry me for some months but could never manage it. She became a well-known journalist, married a young psychologist named Michael Fordham and was killed in enemy action during the last war.

To this epoch also, that is to say the time when any adult woman seemed immensely my superior and senior, belong a number who were distinguished in the arts, the stage or literature. They would probably not have been pleased at the 'senior' bit for several of them were in fact as young as I, but I would not have dreamed of talking to them as equals or juniors. They were to me as Rudyard Kipling and Chesterton had been among men, persons naturally revered by me, whom I felt privileged to meet. Of these were Gertrude Lawrence, who on a memorable occasion came back to my London flat for supper and insisted on helping

Joseph wash up afterwards; poor old G. B. Stern who eventually died of obesity; and the wonderful Baroness Von Hutten who wrote the 'Pam' novels and, seeing a certain young actor (of those days) on the stage, decided that she would make him her lover, and did so. I was fond of Pam and delighted when she remembered our friendship well enough to write to me from Austria just after the Second World War.

Nor can I ever feel anything but a respectful junior to Crystal, the daughter of A. P. Herbert, though I have known and loved her as a friend for twenty years. I used to feel that way too about Malachi Whitaker, the gifted short story teller who was living proof that honour exists among writers. I had conceived the title of a future short story from Suckling's verse—'The Devil Take Her'. Malachi coveted this and instead of quietly appropriating it, she offered me £5 for it, whereas almost any other writer in those impecunious days for all of us would have used it without leave. I read of her death a week or two ago and was saddened by it, and wonder now why I refused the five pounds.

Of these, too, was a woman explorer named Lady Dorothy Mills on a visit to whom I brought a tortoise, and carrying it in my pocket, released it in her drawing-room, swearing in an attempt at eccentricity that I always carried it about with me. I remember her as a kind and elegant woman, not at all like her Press likeness as an intrepid explorer of jungles. Then I met—but did not know intimately—women writers whom I admired, Rebecca West, Rose Macauley, Pamela Frankau and Dorothy Richardson, all of whose books I collected until the point when I parted with most of my books, since I could no longer afford to move them from place to place and country to country in the 1960s. With them in contrast I count the 'persons of stage and screen', as we are told to nominate them now— Molly Daubeny, Hermione Gingold, one of the few women of today who deserves the eighteenth-century title of a wit, Moyra Lubbock, Alida Valli, Estelle Winwood, and Hermione Baddely to whom I owe deep gratitude for one remark, supremely *à propos*, unforgettably comforting, witty and kind, which at a certain crisis gave me entirely new courage and assurance. At a party arranged by my friends for the day of my release from prison, she said, 'Oh dear—more parties. This is the first of so many Coming-Out parties we shall have this year.'

A few more intimately appreciated women friends belong to my adult life, in several cases but not always the wives of men who transcend that category. Berta Ruck, for instance, who was a best-selling novelist in her own right, married Oliver Onions, a writer of note and consequence whose work I have loved and re-read many times. Marguerite McBey, a dear friend in Tangier, who was the widow of the painter and etcher James McBey; Ada Galsworthy, who was kind to me at the awkward age of twenty-two, was, of course, John Galsworthy's beloved wife; Renée Warnford-Davies was the wife of a remarkable industrialist; Gertrude Peppercorn, she herself a fine pianist, was the wife of a very talented if now forgotten writer named Stacey Aumonier; Yolande Donlan, a woman I have loved for her sense of humour; Anna McKew, for her beauty and gift of intimate and sometimes scandalous conversation; all the Rosaire girls of the family with which I tented; Daphne Fielding, who had been the wife of the Marquess of Bath and when I knew her in Tangier was Mrs Xan Fielding.

How can I end this category which I started only to prove myself innocent of the crime (as it is considered today) of misogyny? It is impossible to complete. Ladies of distinction, girls of loveliness and charm, friends who have laughed with me at the absurdity of the world and who have shared with me the love of words pretentiously called literature, wives and mothers of my male comrades, those who have laughed at me and with me as we tried to grow up together, those who have shared my religion and scorned what passed for my politics, girls who with a single smile can light up the grey of a troubled time or who with an illogical assertion can bring down a mountain of cocksure theory, or women who hate the shrill pretentiousness of others as much as I do—they are all crowded round the recollected highways of my past, waiting to be recalled and greeted with affection by the elderly man who writes these words. Most of them have already appeared in one of these books, and desire no more. So alive or dead, now I shall let them rest. Though wait—I must remember dear Julia Killick who spent glorious days with me at Kentish auction sales buying antiques, and Dawn Oliver, my cousin's wife, and that passionate gardener who was the wife of the Madeira ship-owner and writer John Blandy, or Marjorie and Pat Allen of Tangier, or Mariann Rougvie, a dear person and the wife of my only Canadian friend, Cameron Rougvie, or Marguerite, the wife of my lifelong friend Robert Cahiza, or Pamela, the wife of my friend of thirty years' standing, Miles Eadon, or Gwen, wife of my Anglo-Chinese friend Clifford, or more sentimentally little Mary with whom I danced and revelled when I was stationed in Kelso during the war, or Uretta Branch with whom I shared the 'parties' of the 1930s, or dear Maggie Genn, the wife of the distinguished actor Leo, or Jessie Hunslet who befriended me in Zululand, or Viola Hall, or Sheila Ingram.

'A Group of Noble Dames' indeed, or 'Ladies Gay' as I called them in the misunderstood title of a book. I cannot, of course, pretend that every woman I met has been lovable and remembered as an image of loveliness. I have had my antipathetic moments, as what man however romantic has not?

But occasional antipathy is a personal thing and should not be mistaken for misogyny in any sense. Even the most rabid anti-sex discriminator cannot blame a man for disliking some women. The women I have loved, revered or simply respected remain for ever a Group of Noble Dames.

Ten

English Life

As a repatriated emigrant who has spent more than half of his adult life abroad, I feel I should be able to draw some conclusions or make some comparisons, not merely of the town and district in which I have chosen to live, but about life in England considered generally and about the English people and their ways, from which I have been separated during all the fourteen years I lived on the Mediterranean. 'What do they know of England who only England know?' asked Kipling with an eye (one could swear) to *The Oxford Dictionary of Quotations*. Perhaps I can claim an even closer intimacy—born in Kent, brought up in a stockbroker's happy family in the Home Counties, educated at Tonbridge, a self-consciously conventional English Public School, occupied in writing all my life, I have been very much aware of my Englishness, though determined to talk colloquially in Spanish, French, German, Italian, Urdu, and in the little that remains of Romanes. (I remember during the war giving Romanes among the languages I knew and nearly finding myself dropped by parachute in Romania—MI5 having supposed that the tongue of the gypsies was the language of that country.) So it was that although I was rarely mistaken for an Englishman in foreign lands, I remained markedly, even typically, English in many respects among my fellow countrymen.

Now that I had come home to roost, as it were, I was able to distinguish not only their way of life as compared with that of other Europeans but also the ways in which it had changed since I had lived here for more than three months at a time in 1953, nearly a quarter of a century ago.

There were several marked changes that had been brought about by laws, sometimes beneficent, more often inept. To me and to friends of mine, the Sexual Offences Act of 1967 was the first of these. It removed that fatuous anomaly by which a man who expressed physical affection towards another could, if a blackmailer or policeman wanted to take advantage of it, be sent to prison. The Sexual Offences Act, for which gratitude is owed to Leo Abse, did away with the worst of these abuses and cut down to size such loud-mouthed bigots as the late Lords Montgomery, Kilmuir and Goddard and, understandably, Baden-Powell, the Chief Scout. The effect of the Act in other respects was not as great as these had foreseen. There was no Victory Parade of homosexuals as predicted by their friends in the popular Sunday Press, no beatification for the famous fallen like Wilde and Lord Arthur Somerset, no sign of the Cleveland Street Martyrs, or Last Post for Generals Gordon, Kitchener and Hector Macdonald, or even posthumous decoration for writers like Somerset Maugham, Hugh Walpole and E. M. Forster. There was in fact no public reaction to the law which eradicated the evil practices of the last half century, and in public conduct the only noticeable sign of it has been the relief shown among decent-minded men and women who have studied the question at all. I personally, in 'declaring my interest' in this matter, must make the point that the way in which I was intended to suffer turned out, in the end, happily for me.

It may also be interesting to me, if not to anyone else, to quote the words I wrote in the weeks immediately following the party my friends arranged for the day of my release.

'I am glad it has all happened. Of that I am quite certain now, and I have thought with care and detachment before I make that seemingly preposterous claim. I have had no more than a glimpse into the desolate inferno of prison life because six months give a man, as experienced prisoners say, scarcely time to take his boots off. But for what I have seen and heard and felt I am truly thankful. I have learnt more than I should have done in a decade of free living. I have observed human nature at its best and worst. I understand things which would otherwise have baffled me till I died. I have gained immeasurably and if I have lost anything it is no more than a little superfluous weight and respectability, both of which I gladly leave behind me. I have realized what pawky-natured and dirty-minded men can do to one who has aroused their jealousy and I have known great courage and nobility in those most bitterly condemned by their fellows. It has been the most immensely worthwhile experience in my life.'

A less happy, indeed a result half painful and half ludicrous, has been another attempt by Government to interfere in the natural behaviour of men and women, the Sex Discrimination Act of the present day. This is a measure which is so insulting to women by reason of the discrimination it seeks to prevent but only succeeds in exaggerating to such monstrous lengths that the very name reduces people to helpless laughter or sullen indignation. Calling a barmaid a 'bar-person' and avoiding the prefix 'woman' to novelists or as a suffix to 'sports' (as in 'sportswoman') will do nothing to increase the wages, prestige, strength or amiability of females in relation to males, rather the contrary, and one questions who in the world could have supposed it would do so. Coming from civilized countries abroad I was staggered to hear that such retrograde legislation was actually on the statute book, and I look forward impatiently to the removal of this imbecility which will surely come. I wait indeed for any attempt to put into practice the more fatuous provisions of this Act and should be pleased if they were used against me. I would not waste a lawyer's time to defend me but act for myself, and try to prove that it is women who would suffer, not only from ridicule but from humiliation, if there was any attempt at prosecution under the Act.

But also if we make the hypothesis that the police could be ordered to further its provisions, we should burden members of the overworked police force yet again, much as we had burdened them before the 'Abse Act' by sending them into public urinals as *agents provacateurs*. They could be called to deal with a shopkeeper who had accidently served a man before a waiting queue of females, or a manager who advertised for 'chorus girls' instead of 'persons of the chorus'. They might have to prosecute cinema owners who spoke of an 'usherette' instead of 'the person with the lamp' or take on the whole Admiralty for not obliterating the W in WRNS. The mind, in a word, boggles at the possibilities if the Sex Discrimination Act should ever be an active part of our system. Words like 'mother', 'wife', 'sister' would have to be among the first to go and 'virility' and 'femininity' would be rude, perhaps actionable words. The only safe adjective to use would be 'neuter' or perhaps in hostile company, 'hermaphroditical'. At any rate, just as the Race Discrimination Act has created more problems for our black population than it has solved, so the Sex Discrimination Act—if anyone takes any notice of it—will do similar things to women. But no one will, of course. Within a year or two it will be seen as the silly anachronism, except in purely economic terms, that it is.

There is one effect for these and similar fads of socialistic theorizing—the extra duties they give to policemen. I do not mean that they—yet, at least—are expected to stop people in the street whom they have overheard talking of barmaids, nursemaids or chorus girls, or that they are any longer asked to wear make-up and earrings to approach men suspected of soliciting, but there are duties which indirectly arise from these and similar anomalies which may distract honest coppers from their primary duties of preventing crime.

Mugging, for instance. One would suppose that a town like Bournemouth with a reputation as a haven for retired 'senior citizens' (as the cant phrase goes) would be fairly free from the young highwaymen who infest large manufacturing cities, but the supposed 'one' would be gravely mistaken. In the first place, towns of similar repute, Cheltenham, Tunbridge Wells and Bath for instance, nearly all have a district noted for violence, crime and vice, and in the second place Bournemouth, with its many public gardens open at all hours, has more mugging than can even reach police files. I have not so far been the victim of this, even though I provide what is an open invitation to muggers by unavoidably walking with the limp and stick of an obviously elderly man, but that mugging—and sometimes dangerously violent mugging—goes on frequently in the summer I know by report, officially from newspapers which give prominence to such cases, and privately from common information. In the week before writing this it was called 'highway robbery' when a Spanish waiter was attacked and robbed in one of our quiet and well-laid-out public gardens.

The police dedicated to the prevention of violent political crime by explosion and kidnapping must be congratulated on their remarkable success in a particularly difficult task, and there is no reason to suppose that other policemen would not have done as well against petty criminals and other lawbreakers if they were not perpetually called off to chase motorists whose licences are out of date or tyres are outworn, arrest streakers or go in numbers to relieve the victims of so-called pickets, to protect politicians from their vociferous opponents or pursue youngsters using borrowed cars. I do not begrudge the most junior of policemen their salaries, though they earn far more by investigating minor offences than I can earn by writing of murder for a reading public of several thousand free subscribers to lending libraries, but I would like them to be given a chance to arrest young villains whose idea of a joke combined with profit is to attack the elderly and infirm for the usually meagre sums they may be carrying, and making the streets of British suburbia less safe than the medinas of Tangier or

Algiers, the red-light districts of Hamburg or Amsterdam, or the Mafia-infested slums of great cities everywhere.

This is one of the difficulties of living in almost any region of Great Britain and is a thing which—in a detestable cliché—'we have to learn to live with'.

Another is the talk and practice of drug-taking. After living in Tangier for fourteen years I speak with some authority on the effects of this and have seen too many cheerful and intelligent young people reduced to vacant imbecility from indulging in the taking of marihuana (*kif*) to listen to the dangerous idiots who say that there is 'no harm in it' or that 'it is not habit-forming'. It is admittedly not as body- and mind-destroying as one of the 'hard' drugs which give nothing of sensation or imagination, only a perpetual craving for relief through another dose and another as each wears off, an eternity of nothingness until life ends or in the rarest of cases until the craving is relieved by another, usually no less harmful, drug taken in larger quantities.

That drug-taking of both varieties, minor and major, is practised in Great Britain and Ireland there can be little doubt, often initiated among schoolchildren by their 'daring' one another, or experimenting, or by conversion by others lately converted. It can only be fought among the young by contrary but not dissimilar means—ridicule, contempt for cowardliness and the conviction publicly expressed that 'pushers' are the most despicable of creatures. Among the mature, a few heroic men and women fight for long and sometimes hopeless periods to produce an occasional 'cure', but even that is unreliable and subject to reversion. All this has come to pass in Great Britain almost (though not entirely) during the last two decades. Although I find it easy to exclude it, or any thought of it, from my own life and that of Joseph, I cannot be unaware that in coming to make my home in this country I am among people who either practise some form of drug-taking themselves or 'have learned to live with it' in others.

I do not allow that in this there is any room for the 'tolerance', 'broad-mindedness' or understanding which are so popular among clerics and other television speakers today. I have no use for any of these synonyms for habitual and suicidal weakness. A modicum of pity is all I allow myself to feel for these victims; I cheerfully suffer for this all the opprobrious adjectives that may be bestowed on me —I am bigoted, prejudiced, a monster of cramped ideas and cruelty. Usually so permissive and easy-going in my ideas, in this I become an opinionated doctrinaire, if not a plain fool. *Everyone* knows that *kif* is harmless and that laws against it should be thrown out. Here's one exception. I feel unrepentantly prohibitive, and shall remain so.

As for handbag-snatching and other forms of theft, they are surely symptomatic of a more universal malaise. Last summer I left the French windows open into my bedroom in a particularly warm spell, and noticed two small boys, of ten and eight years I would suppose, wandering along the patio, apparently looking for a way to reach the back of the house. I thought no more of it after they had unhurriedly walked down the steps to the road. Then going into my bedroom I found that five or six little carved animals which Joseph had given me to decorate the top of a chest of drawers were missing. It was a good example of a cool and purposeful crime, carried out with finesse and probably after some practice, though the gear was of little commercial value.

I do not believe that if anyone else had seen those two neatly dressed open-faced small boys, they would have suspected them of entering the open ground around these flats, visible from the road and from other windows, with the deliberate intention of picking up anything they could lay their hands on, as they undoubtedly did. The point is that they must have discussed the possibilities together and probably with others, and that thus are criminals made. All they need is a few years of practice and challenge and they will begin a hard professional career. Whose fault will that be? Mine, perhaps for leaving the door open? Their parents' for condoning or even encouraging them? The police's for not catching them? The magistrates' for treating them too lightly or too severely? Anyone's but their own, goes the modern dictum, which prefers 'Society' as a scapegoat to the natural thievishness of a pair of young rascals. Perhaps that is right. Perhaps 'we all' are to blame, a comforting but evasive solution. It was never Oliver but always the Artful Dodger or Fagin or Bill Sykes who was the guilty one.

Criminals are made, like most other people and things, by *conversation*. When those two little wretches meet their friends and show them the gear they have snatched and laughingly boast of their achievement, they may make a sneak-thief of anyone who hears them, just as a swaggering drunk makes a convert (whether he means to do so or not) of a potential alcoholic who hears him tell of the six pints he consumed last night without a hiccup. Some day people may learn that words are the most powerful agents in life, spoken, written or sung.

Was it always so? I daresay, but the particular wordy contempt for the forces of Law and Order, the anecdotes of 'how I made a fool of the police' and of 'our village copper' date chiefly from the years immediately after the last war when the Force was both rotten and arrogant. I am the first to admit that after saying hard things of them in the past, I sympathize with them now in their difficulties. It is one thing to call themselves 'Police Officers', quite another to gain respect from the law-abiding among the population. But if I had not learnt to respect and like them now, I should have done so in any case after I had seen the ridiculously self-important oafs who form the police force of nearly every Mediterranean nation. We may not think our policemen are 'wonderful' in the old popular term, but compared with Spanish, Moroccan, Cypriot and all the rest (including Maltese and Libyan), they are models of civility and justice. So it is that in spite of the present wave of lawlessness justified by general anti-establishmentism, a popular form of spurious anarchy, I have no regrets on this score for having returned to England. I even have friends among the police, a thought impossible to me twenty years ago when I wrote of them in *The Quest for Quixote* as 'members of the most contemptible profession in the world', a phrase which Alfred Knopf asked me to delete in the American edition.

It is all very well to talk of the Police Force as worthy or corrupt; there is a doubt relative to that which every man who faces the question to himself must sooner or later ask —how honourable, or should we say how honest, can he claim to have been himself throughout a varied lifetime? Perhaps you may think that it does not matter very much and that there are qualities far more important than what one may call commercial honesty, but since we all claim to possess it and feel that we are superior to thieves, confidence tricksters, swindlers and blackmailers, it is a question very well worth discovering the truth about, and answering to one's own searching questions. To those of us in middle and later age who were brought up by Victorian parents, there can be little or no excuse for dishonesty, since it would run counter to all we learnt in childhood—and all we have loved in our heroes.

I remember at the age of seven or so being told by my father that all the dealings on the Stock Exchange were by word of mouth, instantly accepted and trusted, and only later confirmed in writing by clerks in offices. It may have been a somewhat rosy picture of the Stock Exchange but I had no doubt then or now that it was true of men like my father or the friends of his whom I met with him in Throgmorton Street, Messrs Shearing, Carvalho, Lazarus and Jefferies, my uncle Edward Taylor and my cousin Hugh Shelbourne. So far as I remember, that conversation with my father kept me strictly honest until I became a dealer in old books and first editions, when competition in sharp dealing became too much for me and I learnt a great deal about books as well as their appearances, prices and dates. I do not think I have ever been a dishonest person by category but I have been satisfied with the standard of honesty attained by my fellows. That in the high-principled days of the past would certainly not have been considered enough.

That I and the vast majority of middle- and working-class men have never stolen is a poor claim to make, since stealing by even the professionals is a matter of simply weighing the possibility of success against that of retribution, so that the more barefaced robbers are frequently those who are less often punished, and stealing, considered in a twisted and immoral way, might be called a test of courage. Consider the various ways in which E. W. Hornung tried (and failed) to excuse the inexcusable conduct of Raffles. Consider that among all those who have abused Oscar Wilde, the one really blameworthy act of his life, his marriage with Constance Lloyd's sufficient income, is rarely mentioned.

I sadly conclude, after three years in my own country, that honesty is cheap and honour appears in rare and notable cases, unseen by the majority of citizens, and celebrated only in old-fashioned verse and drama. If one really wants to be sententious and boring about it, one may conclude that both those related qualities, honesty and honour, disappeared with the British Empire and with the men who were trained for its administration and the women who loved and admired them. But as for the famous swindlers, I think they are spaced out through English history, though they are better noticed and reported in this age of the 'media'. I can remember seeing from the top of a tram an ugly suburban house with a cultivated garden, in Norwood I think, and hearing my father remark that 'old Hobbes' lived there—apparently a famous swindler. I heard too of Jabez Balfour and later of Horatio Bottomley and Clarence Hatry, who in a sense published a novel of mine. In our own time we have had Poulson and those connected with him and, as I write this, we are promised some more big-time crooks. None of them seems to indicate a change for the worse or better, and Members of Parliament, town councillors, charity organizers and commercial tycoons turn up as leaders of some mighty embezzlement at fairly regular intervals in time, and do not seem to be of much interest to the historian. More significant than these publicized peculations by men who were, or who soon became, familiar to the public at large, are the petty criminals who chatter of their offences—'Had a bit of bovver with the Law last night', 'Seen those watches Jack nicked last week?', 'Going spade-bashing tonight. Like to come?'—familiar words in many town pubs, spoken loudly and with pride. These certainly have increased among most age-groups since I left England in 1954.

Another great change from the time when I lived in England last is the more sensible attitude of the English to the black population. It is no thanks to the bumbling and damaging efforts of succeeding governments to introduce laws intended to prevent so-called racial discrimination which, like those against sex discrimination, are dangerous and divisive, that people have learned to behave in a civilized and natural way with immigrants. I can sense this through the experience of Joseph, who has never since he came from the Tamilian area of India been made aware of one suggestion of prejudice or deliberate discourtesy here. It may be because he has a humorous way of turning away any sign of these, saying 'I've been working like a *black* today', or using other phrases like 'a touch of the tar-brush' and generally making an adversary feel like a character in *Love Your Neighbour*, but it is also because the ill-bred boorishness of racialism has, like Enoch Powell, almost disappeared from public life.

Even here in Bournemouth, a city teeming with North African and other foreign students who come to learn English, very little animosity is felt for them; indeed they seem to dislike one another far more than they dislike or are disliked by the English, in spite of their tendency to ponce.

There are other advantages in English life which one does not notice on first acquaintance. It costs less than life abroad, especially for an Englishman who has most of the tastes and necessities of his own country, as I have. Not only in food, which I have discussed, but in the many little things we take for granted here and which abroad are obtained only with difficulty, imported or regarded as luxuries because to the people of the country they are so. I am only too much aware of the absurdity of collecting

Green Shield and other stamps, and swear that I will never stand in a queue for an hour to obtain a parcel of almost valueless glassware which I neither need nor want, yet I find myself actually unable to throw the wretched things away. I know the falsity of the whole system of claiming that a purchaser saves a sum of money by buying something which is supposed to have 'thirty pence off' or on the promise that a £5,000 holiday with all expenses paid *must* be won by one of the lucky purchasers, when none of the things offered is really needed or really wanted by any sane window- or magazine-page shopper. I know all this, yet I look through advertisements with all the other zany victims of clever salesmen. I even occasionally, though most infrequently, follow instructions to 'send post free' but with a cheque or postal order enclosed to obtain something I am assured is a special or once-in-a-century offer which I shall regret to the end of my life having missed. I am a sucker for special reductions in the price of liquor, though I know that brand whisky, for instance, can only be sold fourpence or fivepence below the standard price, for cash as opposed to credit, by a vendor with a big cash business. These are English tricks—or special offers, if you like—almost unknown in the countries in which I have been living. I well remember some weekly journal offering a unique prize to the winner of a competition—no less than the star Phyllis Monkman as a wife! Whether that offer was ever fulfilled I do not remember but it was made in bold letters some time before the First World War. So bargains and promises that you can be rich if you enter a competition are not something new. I look at them all. The sheer silliness of it attracts me, and I am reminded of an exotic character in Tangier, now deceased, called Ziggi the One. He was a renegade former British Civil Servant in West Africa who wrote, as a famous and reliable witch-doctor, lively articles in a Freetown publication on how to rid oneself of a mother-in-law or mosquitoes, and inserted advertisements in the same offering the unique and magical services of Ziggi the One. African subscribers eagerly sent postal orders for Ziggi the

One's Inexhaustible Purse—'However much you take out it can never be empty'—and he received a steady stream of paper money to secure information on how to put a curse on one's enemies or an infallible spell on would-be loved ones. He grew alarmed one day when he discovered that he was advising a Senior Government Minister on steps to be taken when a recalcitrant sister-in-law was in his way, but usually his business ran smoothly and profitably. His methods were at least more original than those of the man who simply answered 'Do what I'm doing' to enquirers about 'How to make a thousand a year in your spare time'.

But to my mind the most vicious form of plundering simple folk is the use of the word SAVE where its opposite SPEND is really intended. 'Save £4' on an article of furniture or of household necessity often means 'Buy this article (which you may not really want or need) for £18 when it has been sold or advertised by another firm at £22, or is actually worth or could be imported at that sum. This is worked from the most expensive and least useful things like washing-machines or motor-cars to the cheapest like soap-powder or breakfast cereal, from magazines professedly showing you how to buy more cheaply or after-shave lotion claiming to provide 'all the perfumes of Arabia', 'a stream of rich distilled perfumes' at a few pence a spray. I immediately turn away from a newspaper or switch off commercial telvision when I am bidden in a shopkeeper's whining imperative to SAVE so much, knowing it means precisely the opposite.

There are other aspects of this seaside town of middle-class England in which I have chosen to live which differ from the other places or times I have known. I re-member my mother plaintively asking her friends or relations after the First World War 'Where *have* all the *nice* people gone?' I expect I thought that an appalling piece of class-conscious snobbery but I knew exactly what she meant and would know again today if a pre-war anachron-istic person asked the same question. The fact that I prefer the people who have been thrown up to the surface by the tide of standardization to the 'ladies and gentlemen' I remember as my parents' friends in childhood is fortunate but of no social significance. There are few *nice* people' as my mother observed, but I don't miss them and have always chosen my friends from the most plebeian or eccentric or foreign or odd of the population. Not so, Joseph. Coming from a culture many centuries older than ours, he is more conscious than I am of the refinement or otherwise of our friends. What both of us loathe is pretentiousness, just as my father and mother did, though they used both to call it 'vulgarity'. I am afraid that a good deal of this can be laid at the charge of the advocates of Women's Lib. For instance I still find it offensive when a woman smokes in the street or a man flourishes a pipe in the presence of women, especially when he is being televised, and I cannot help following a habit which I learned in Argentina fifty years ago of removing my hat in a lift when women are in it, or 'walking on the outside' as my mother taught me to do. I am conscious of being a 'square' in these performances but I prefer to be old-fashioned rather than what was called ignorant in my youth.

Bournemouth is not an ill-mannered town—rather the contrary, but it has its proportion of ferocious mums shoving the less aggressive out of the way and of youngsters with an ill-bred coarseness—or is it is exhibitionism? —showing off loudly in the street. It has its proportion, too, of charming and courteous young folk, as I have discovered now that I am slow-moving and lame. And in neither of these extremes has England changed noticeably since I was a boy, a young man, or a soldier.

One might in fact lump a whole lot of factions and issues under 'politics' to see that it has changed scarcely at all fundamentally. Paying most of what one has earned or inherited to 'save the country' or 'keep down inflation' may be 'a good thing' (only a skilled political economist has any right to an opinion on that) but it certainly was not what our fathers and still less our grandfathers would have consented to. Nor would they have cared to have small illnesses attended to by a state doctor while nothing is remedied that needs such an operation as one for hernia or prostate gland on the grounds that there are no vacancies for two years or more, whatever the suffering occasioned. Nor do I think they would actually have purred with pleasure had they been given notice to quit the home they had occupied for a generation or two in order that a road could be widened or a block of flats built. Most elderly people feel a mite hard-done-by when they learn (without having any option in the matter) that the vast sums collected from them in rates are to be spent on an improved free diet to the children of 'workers' who are paid or subsidized more highly than they are, while they use not only their physical but their mental energies, sometimes for undetermined hours. The only feeble consolation we have for these and many other anomalies is to consider them as the faults of 'politics', of Wilson or Heath, Benn or Thatcher, and decide not to vote for anyone at the next election. Since every party elected is to blame for some hideous blunder, the only way to avoid guilt is not to vote at all, however tempted we may feel to vote *against* someone or other.

Eleven

Writing

How easily I could make this book (in which I am recalling some early experiences) one of those essays in self-pity, one of those complaints of cruelties suffered in childhood and injustices in manhood which are so popular as the auto-biographies of writers and successful artists of all kinds. The materials are ready, some of them viciously etched and promising to produce boyhood sufferings which left notable scars in later life. It would go something like this. I was isolated by three years from the older part of the large family into which I was born, I was bullied by my second brother, Bertie, who was held up to me as a hero when he became a Captain in the R.F.C. in the First World War. I was 'too old' for my younger brothers and separated by the great gulf of sex from my sister. My mother had no under-standing of me and consequently was permanently sus-picious and jealous of my every action, and my father, though kind and understanding, was limited and at the same time forceful in his views and principles. My education was mixed. I was sent as a boarder to a preparatory school with a shameless sadist as the proprietor at the age of less than seven years, under the care of my eldest brother Ronald who was so weak-minded that he relied on me, five years his junior, for support. I was sent to Tonbridge as a day-boy at eleven years old, taught Greek on 'the Classical side' and so loathed it that I made no progress at all. Leaving Tonbridge because my father wanted to move to Eastbourne, I was sent as a boarder to a Dotheboys Hall called Aldenham because my mother's hearty brothers had survived it. Expelled (fortunately) from there for telling a dirty story to a day-boy, I was sent to Wellington College, Salop, not as we had to explain *the* Wellington College, but now called Wrekin College. No member of the staff knew Greek, so it was dropped from my syllabus, meaning (in those days) loss of any chance of going to Oxford. I left it at a low point in my father's fortunes and (at seventeen) became a preparatory schoolmaster, starting at seventy pounds a year.

Every detail of that is accurate, yet what a monstrously false picture it paints. It leaves out, to start with, the two women who gave me grace and understanding in childhood, Ninna and Miss Wain. Percy Browning, the headmaster of Rose Hill School in Banstead, *was* a sadist, a Eurasian Rowing Blue who had married a queen of snobbery. She kept the school together by charming the wealthier parents and fussing over their sons. But I had as happy a time there as any small boy away from home at that age. And of Tonbridge I was immensely proud, and life in the area on a seven-hundred-acre farm of woods and a rushing stream was wholly delightful to me. At Wellington, Salop, I appreciated that grand old monster, John Bayley, and though I formed one of the few invincible hatreds in my life for the unspeakable 'vice-principal' Dobson, a drunken pederast of revolting habits, I learned in exchange to have real feeling for Shakespeare and literature in general from a genius of his kind, Walter Howarth. As for teaching in preparatory schools, little could be of such a senseless waste of time for the unfortunate young men, underpaid, given grossly inadequate accommodation and food, but regarded as having one of the only jobs in which the 'sons of gentlemen' could occupy themselves before finding some way in which what talents they had could be used, an apotheosis which never came to some of them. In its early years my boyhood does not compare in brutality with that of Rudyard Kipling, but in its later times when I obtained a teaching post in Buenos Aires I was given the same opportunities to learn and write as he had in India (or as Isherwood had in

Berlin, for that matter), though not having the youthful genius of either of them I failed to take advantage of it.

I could continue in this two-sided vein right through my life but do not see what use the exercise would have since I could convince no one, least of all myself, that I had not spent a gloriously happy time from childhood to old age. There have been misfortunes and periods of sadness, but only enough of them to give lively contrasts in the whole pattern. That does not mean that I have been successful; I imagine that the majority of mankind who counts success in terms of income or status achieved would judge me to be remarkably unsuccessful, a failure in the accumulation both of money and honours. To this I reply in all modesty that I disagree. I have largely done whatever I wanted, achieved as much as I think I have deserved, and enjoyed, in different ways, every decade of my life. I have never been bored, and if anyone remembers that I said I was, I give him or her notice that I was lying, or claiming for a moment a spasm of *ennui* caused by some bull-headed egotist or merely being insulting to my hearers during a fit of exasperation.

When it comes to my professional career, that is to say (more simply) my progress as a writer, it is a different picture. I really think I can claim—though still I hope without self-pity—more than a normal mass of misfortunes, mixed with just enough spots of good luck to keep the whole endurable. Throughout childhood I 'lisped in numbers' which I took seriously enough to do what most young scribblers and a few poets have done—collect my verse into books which by one means or another I published, one collection being issued in eccentric type by Victor Neuburg, the Vickybird of the Vine Press, Steyning, Sussex, and another by my lifelong friend, Lincoln Torrey Brown, the younger brother of Richard, who was born in the same week as I was and died two years ago. I went as a totally unqualified schoolmaster to Buenos Aires and during my two years there published piles of verse in an English newspaper and in a little monthly paper which I published and edited myself with my friend 'Bimbo' Beccar

Varela, son of the country's most eminent lawyer—a position he has now inherited himself. Returning to England I settled down in a disused army hut in a Kentish plum orchard and for three years lived by little cheques from editors—sometimes as small as 10/- for a poem or an article—the total reaching £120 or £150 a year, on which I subsisted. When J. C. Squire, Harold Monro and Harriet Monro of *Poetry* Chicago published my poems I thought I had achieved something until T. S. Eliot and his followers swept away all the little Neo-Georgians like me. My first novel was published by Arthur Waugh, Evelyn's father and Alec's, who was director of Chapman and Hall. It was kindly, almost fulsomely, reviewed but sold six hundred copies, netting me £30 to pay agent (£3), typist (£4) and living expenses during the six months I spent on it (£23). I was paid £60 for my next novel (*Night Out*) but it meant my being published by Walter Hutchinson, over the doors of whose offices during his lifetime should have been a sign 'Abandon Hope All Ye Who Enter Here'. (He lived up to this himself a few years later, committing suicide just after the Second World War.)

Then came for me what seemed to be success but turned out to be a calamity. Living in Barcelona on forty pesetas a week (then about £2) in a smart little hotel, I wrote a long novel named *Cosmopolis*. In it I brought together a rich crowd of eccentrics on a Swiss mountain and enjoyed their antics as Compton Mackenzie and Norman Douglas had enjoyed watching the cosmopolitans of Capri. The book had absurdly indulgent reviews and seemed set for best-sellerdom. But the proprietor of a school on a Swiss mountain for whom I had worked for a time arrived in London to claim that my book libelled him, and frightened Hutchinson into withdrawing it.

I had no means of fighting this and lost all earnings of the book. But that was only the beginning of disaster. Hutchinson claimed from me all the losses he had suffered, and persuaded me to sign a contract agreeing to write *four books a year* until the amount was paid off. (I keep a copy of this unbelievable contract as a souvenir of the time in which I would have starved but for the kindness of two good women, Julia Killick and her daughter Joan.) Nor was that all. The book had been sold to Lincoln McVeagh in America but Hutchinson warned him and he in turn withdrew it. Then as I was beginning to recover from these body-blows I received a telegram from Carl Laemmle offering me £1,500 for the film rights of the same book. This seemed to compensate for everything, and I passed several weeks spending the money in imagination—this in my needy and hungry state was not difficult to do—until I heard from my agents (who would or could do nothing about it) that Tallulah Bankhead, for whom the story was intended, did not like the book and the offer was withdrawn.

I was twenty-seven years old then and in the next five years I turned out, at the expense of any decent writing I might have done, no less than ten novels in fulfilment of that iniquitous contract, although I did my best to stick to my principle of writing as well as I was capable of doing. At last I felt strong enough to say 'enough is enough' and made new terms with Hutchinson and started to write what I wanted to. But even that was not the end of Hutchinson. After the war when I thought all contracts with him had run out and I had signed up with another firm, he waited until my new book was about to come out and then issued an older book in the same month, thereby damaging the fresh start I hoped to make. I sued him for breach of contract but it was in the Chancery Court and he employed a famous Q.C., Sir Valentine Holmes, and won the case, threatening to bankrupt me if I failed to pay the whole amount of his costs. Is it remarkable that I hoped when he killed himself that he did not shuffle off his mortal coil without some degree of misery?

Looking back I see that my problem was not the *way* I wrote during those half-wasted years but the choice of subject I was forced to make when I might have been establishing myself as my contemporaries were doing with steady progress at the time. But I have to admit that it was, as I began by saying, a loss to me professionally and in no way spoiled the late twenties and thirties of my life. I lived in the Cotswolds for most of that time and made voyages to Buenos Aires and Europe, and had all the happiness recalled in *The Wild Hills*.

After that, in the years since the Second World War, my misfortunes in the jealous world of literature, compared with those of my early years, appear almost insignificant. I have suffered from my share of bankrupt publishers and dishonest agents, but no more than other writers, like those who trusted the publisher Smithers or the agents Pinker long, or not so long ago. The book I thought nearest to a potential best-seller, *Wilkie*, was damned by its publishers, Macdonald, who wrote that they 'could not think it would have much success among so many thousand Socialist voters', although Somerset Maugham made it his Book of the Year in the *Sunday Times*. An agent lost me the verbal contract which that dear old man, the Aga Khan, had made with me to write his biography, and although I have been published by a dozen American publishers, each of whom promised that he meant to make me successful, they have all grown tired of the effort after issuing one or two books without instantly topping charts. Most writers have suffered from one or another of these things, but few have done so while being unfailingly industrious all the time, as I have. And of course we all, every professional or amateur writer among us, suffer from the patently unjust and apparently eternal procrastination of each succeeding government brought face to face with the cruelty and deprivation caused by their failure to implement a Public Lending Right.

I do not, I repeat, pity myself for all these disasters. I sometimes get bloody angry, but count them all as the natural consequences of an otherwise richly rewarded profession.

Disaster of another kind came in my first year in Bournemouth, as I have recounted in Chapter Five, for when I first felt the effects of the stroke which took away my power to walk I found, on Easter Saturday (the stroke having come appropriately on Good Friday), that I was unable to guide a pen, even to the signing of my name. To most present-day writers this would have mattered little for they can type or dictate their way through a novel quite easily and swiftly. It was not so with me. From my very first efforts till that Eastertime I had never done anything but *write* my work, and not until the late 1930s did I even use a fountain pen, preferring Relief nibs and penholders. To find that I could not write, in the literal sense, was therefore a serious blow, particularly as for some weeks I had no reason to think that facility would ever return. I arranged with my bank for Joseph to sign cheques for me and took seriously my two hours a week under a physiotherapist and hoped for the best.

I have before this confirmed that having been born under the sign of Gemini, when misfortune comes to me it is never at its worst, and after about two months I began to make ungainly scribbles which, however, were intelligible to Joseph, and although I can no longer cover long pages with my firm swinging handwriting, I am writing this book and making it decipherable to Joseph.

It is just as well that I found these remedies, for, as I have related earlier, a 'phone call from Jeffrey Simmons, my publisher, set me to work again. Altogether I was pretty pleased with *Conduct Unbecoming: A Novel by Rupert Croft-Cooke* as its title-page proclaimed, though I felt a touch of misrepresentation when I thought how much I owed to Barry England, the author of the play, and Robert Enders, who had written the screenplay. However, it was issued both in paperback and hardback and sold a great many thousand copies and meant that I remained 'in work' during that disastrous year. Moreover, the efforts I had to make to get its words down on paper were invaluable in habituating my right hand to penmanship, and although I can never produce a page of manuscript as before, I can *write*, which, as they say, is something. To do so creatively is a painful and laborious business, and I remember nostalgically running again and again across the sheets of lined paper which I have used since my schooldays, 120 words to a quarto page or 250 words of typescript on one of the same size, but I *can write* when I have the physical energy and am doing so now at two lines a minute, so that I have fairly good hopes of finishing this book and with it the series that has occupied me (with one or two other things) for the last twenty years.

Has it been worthwhile? I have not the slightest idea and I do not intend to ponder over that question. Perhaps after an atomic war when half humanity with its culture and history has been wiped out, there may be some inquisitive researcher studying life in the twentieth century with all its triviality and old-fashioned ideas of progress to whom this series, discovered under several tons of more important bibliographia, might be welcome as lighter reading while he goes wearily through the egomaniac mass of autobiography of this century. Perhaps not. I have enjoyed writing it, anyway, and think of myself not unkindly, writing away at my table in Tangier, on a pad at the circular table of the sitting-room in Patrick Kinross's house in Little Venice, London, in that noisy flat on the fifth floor of a block in Las Palmas, beside the fireside in a (then) Greek building in Famagusta in Cyprus, in the great long-shaped room overlooking a busy street in Tunis, looking over an early nineteenth-century garden in the Dublin suburb of Dun Laoghaire, in Ceuta and Melilla, in a Cologne suburb and here in this English flat in which I am glad to have come to rest. I have carried the past with me to all these places and have eagerly re-lived it in all these un-English climates. For the past is so precious to me that I would carry it even farther if I could. Yes, of all things that I shall most regret leaving when the time comes to put away my toys, it is my own past that I shall shut in the cupboard most sulkily as I did that golliwog which one of my godparents had given me at Christmastime when King Edward VII reigned.

As for the poetry I wrote with such assiduity between the ages of eleven and thirty, I have no illusions about its quality, admitting frankly its naivety, derivativeness and tintinnabulation. Yet it is a fact that I can look over it now, forty years later, with far less embarrassment than I feel towards my early fiction, and I believe this is a common experience among writers who have developed in similar ways. The fact is I am fond of some of those poems, perhaps remember nostalgically the circumstances or persons which caused me to write them and although I accept the charge that they are nothing but a late and minor outcrop of 'Georgian Poetry' I do not believe that is such a bad thing to be. This has nothing to do with conceit or inflated self-opinion. I do not admire the poems I wrote—I could in fact write with devastating criticism about them now. But there remains in my mind a genuine affection for them and I am delighted when anyone feels the same. I am not hurt if I am told that they are rubbish or dated or petty, but I am immoderately pleased when someone (as occasionally happens) is familiar with them.

Poetry is the most social form of literature, and great friendships or groups are common among poets. When we do not know much about a poet's friends, associates, rivals or confidants, it only means that we have not studied the facts of his life. We can do no more than guess to whom Chaucer read extracts from his work or who guffawed as he listened to The Miller's Tale read out by the ribald author. We have better ideas about Shakespeare's cronies and can follow the intimate relationships between Byron, Shelley and Keats. Perhaps the poet inherits from his minstrel forbears the necessity to spout his own verse to others of his own, or in the case of the Brownings of the other, sex. For my own part I have had only one associate to whom I have ever read anything, prose or verse, my brother Laurie, who because his knowledge of the Greek and Latin classics was considerable, provided me with a kind of challenge. With others I suppose I was too much out of sympathy to feel interest either in their work or themselves. So far as writing was concerned I was always, and rejoiced in being, a loner. I cannot remember a single intimate conversation about literature since my adolesence when I was all too keen to talk about 'favourite writers', 'great poets' and comparisons with the classics, though even then I do not think I ever discussed my own work, except perhaps in a commercial way with editors or agents, and even today I have absolutely no knowledge of what fellow-writers or even friends think of my work. I feel none of the need for encouragement when I 'get stuck' in the course of a novel as, according to Sheila Kaye-Smith, her contemporary, Francis Brett Young, used to feel. ('He has to send for a Mrs So-and-so from England,' said his wife. 'She can always give him the encouragement to get him going again'. 'But what happens,' asked Sheila naively, 'if she doesn't like it?' The answer has been carried away by the sirocco of Capri.)

I am, I'm afraid, a very workaday writer and have never understood the term 'inspiration'. Perhaps (I realize since I had the inability to form the letters of writing) it simply means good health or reasonably good health without which the effort of a thousand words or so per day cannot be achieved. Perhaps it means facility or inventiveness, or skill in dictation or typewriting, or the gift of laughter-making or rhyming or verbal landscape-painting—one or an accumulation of these perhaps which wins an author acclamation from professional reviewers or public-library clients. At any rate, if I have any of that mysterious quality of 'inspiration' I am quite unaware of it and enjoy just writing away, pausing occasionally to re-read a passage the forming of which I particularly enjoyed.

So that as I have shared the occupation of the earth with a few million others during this century which is coming nearer to its close, and as a number of these must have been dedicated as I have been to the 'pursuit of letters', I imagine that I must be to blame for not seeking them out and sharing literary confidences and ambitions as others have done, deriving comfort and encouragement from joining literary associations or the P.E.N., or the Society of Authors and the rest, or merely making part of a clique around some leader of literary fashions. Unfortunately I am no good at this sort of thing and if I join one of them I resign almost as soon as I get my membership card, so that I no longer bother the hardworking folk who organize them. As a writer, I realize finally, I am unliterary, though as a man I believe I am gregarious, talkative and affectionate.

Twelve

The Patio

In the school stories of my boyhood when *Chums* was my favourite reading and the *Boys' Own Paper* was considered rather pi, all the juvenile characters were remorselessly typed and none more despised than 'the Naturalist'. Even Kipling, I seem to remember, had a dig at him or at the Natural History Society, and as Billy Bunter was gross and greedy whenever he was mentioned, so the student of wild creatures was bespectacled, absurdly didactic, as though he was a young contributor to *The Posthumous Papers of the Pickwick Club*. The image antagonized all the hearty Philistine side of me, and I think with regret now what I might have learned in the three years when I was given the freedom of the seven hundred acres of Cage Farm near Tonbridge (now a building estate for the families of featureless commuters), or when I lived in boyhood on the Sussex Downs. I might have learnt something of the life of the kingfisher before Ron and Rosemary Eastman made their classic studies of it, or of wood-pigeons and red squirrels before the latter became almost extinct in England, or of the breeding habits of rabbits, otters and badgers and a huge variety of wild flowers and trees. I can still smell drying hops and the mushrooms gathered before breakfast to be fried with bacon, and remember roast-potato parties in the oast-houses and watching the last of the wheat being threshed to see the rats scrambling out to their death by the sticks of the threshers when the last of the stack was gathered up. Then, too, I remember the cows being brought in to be milked by the Kentish cowman's familiar call,

'Curp, curp, come-along curp!' and the wooing sound of the wood-pigeons in the fir trees beside the Shipbourne Road. I loved it all and had many lonely adventures in the farmland, many discoveries and many encounters, but I learned very little of what could be called 'Natural History', and though I can recognize the wild flowers found in such plenty then, I remember few of their correct names. The repellent figure of 'the Naturalist' discouraged me from knowledge.

Now that I once again find myself watching from my study windows the little 'bird-sanctuary', or less grandly the 'bird-table', on the patio and its population, I find that although those years produced little of what countrymen call book-learning, I keep a good deal of miscellaneous learning from my childhood and youth, recognizing species far more accurately than most of my contemporaries and taking great pleasure in welcoming each hesitant arrival on the railings or on the thatched bird-table itself. These come in great variety.

In some ways I am surprised at my own ignorance of quite ordinary facts. It took me a whole year round the seasons to realize why I never saw finches or others of their kind during the winter months and to learn by watching how many of our most beloved birds emigrate during the cold weather, and are thus invisible and silent from September till April. I knew this, of course, about swallows, swifts and house martins, but had not realized how many of the more highly coloured birds have the same habit—greenfinches, chaffinches, jays and cuckoos are migrants. All these I recognized on the patio, the cuckoos briefly and rarely, the finches in numbers. This is not to mention that most anomalous and fascinating bird, the robin, who seems to enjoy a hard winter and leaves his tracks in the snow. We have about four robins who call regularly but never in groups or even couples and who severely cut one another if they chance to alight at the same time. I wonder if there is a television feature or a book on the Private Life of the Robin? It could be absorbing to watch or read.

I happen to know from observation one fact about the robin, and although it must be familiar to many ornithologists I cannot find it mentioned in any text-book. The common species in India, though in colour it is identical with the European, differs in having its red patch not on its breast but on its rump, giving scope to humorists in the British Army, who find everything in the East contrary. But I find the peculiarity about our British robins is their watchful friendliness with men. They will sit on a gardener's spade, hoping that insects will be turned up, and one perches on my shoulder or hand when I go out to the patio. He is, of course, looking for the crumbs which I give him rather than showing affection, but it is a pleasant habit of his, all the same.

I find, though I stand to be corrected by anyone who has studied birds more closely than I have, that hostility among them is nearly always shown to members of their own species rather than strangers on the patio—particularly between the collared doves, of which we have a large number who peck swiftly and cleanly through a pile of grain without pausing to look at one another or any human being at hand. Their steady tap-tap continues till the pile is cleared, but if doves from another family venture near, they attack and continue to attack and pursue till they establish ownership of the grain. Why we call doves the birds of peace I cannot think. They are lovely to look at and interesting to watch, but peaceful they are certainly not. We had one rogue bird among ours. He suffered from some deformity of the spine so that he was called Lon Chaney and behaved like a fiend to the other doves who came to feed. What was notable about him apart from his appearance was his vindictiveness. He would not only drive his rivals away but pursue them sometimes nearly a mile to the trees opposite on the far bank of the chine and peck at them viciously if he came near them. But last winter he disappeared—shot, starved or attacked, it is impossible to know, but we see him no more.

The male cuckoo, unlike 'Lon Chaney', and contrary to

his reputation, is a friendly bird and persistently announces himself to be so. His evil reputation comes from the fact that Nature designed his mate to be so prolific that she has to employ as many as ten or a dozen misguided foster-mothers to hatch out and bring up her young in nests around the spot where she first perched on her arrival as an immigrant, and these usurp the living space of her own brood.

The finest account of the tragedy of what is called the cuckoo's nest (though the cuckoo builds none) has been written by W. H. Hudson in *Hampshire Days*. He tells how he and some young friends watched the whole process, how the hen-cuckoo dropped her larger egg among those in a robin's nest, how the bloated and monstrous baby cuckoo kicked out the young robins one after another until only one was left with the flabby intruder. I have never witnessed all this myself but I know that it takes place, as skilful photographers have shown in film. Besides, W. H. Hudson tells me so, and as I owed my first acquaintance with Argentina to reading his *El Ombú*, so his *Hampshire Days* introduced me to the New Forest, and one of the gods in my private Olympus will always be that poverty-stricken lonely man who, though of American parentage, spent his life between the Pampas and the Southern Counties of England. He taught me that many of the processes of Nature are cruel, that is to say they cause pain and terror, but it has taken human ingenuity to invent the most hideous and deliberate cruelty for man's selfish ends, like condemning animals to a lifetime of darkness and incarceration to produce whiter meat or more plentiful eggs. The cuckoo follows her natural instincts, the fox and the wolf kill from hunger and need, but the man from utterly selfish motives. He alone has the hypocrisy to invent and boast of a paradoxically named instrument which he calls a humane killer. He alone, quite early in his history, invented the bird-cage and the mouse-trap. He alone has the imagination to save creatures from suffering and he alone indulges his inhuman tastes. So although the cuckoo throws out the nestlings of other birds to die, it is untrue to say that he is cruel, as a man can be, as Percy Browning was, as all anglers are, though they cover their cruelty with fishing lore, extracts from Izaak Walton, verses about the contemplative man's pastime. (If anglers contemplate anything, it can only be the torture they inflict on the beautiful dappled swimmers in shadowy streams.)

The greatest cruelty of all, it seems to me, is imprisonment, either of animals or human beings. It is mad to talk of the death penalty as though it were a greater punishment than life imprisonment, and only a selfish man guided by personal fastidiousness would do so. Oh yes, it is very *upsetting* to read of someone being hanged by the neck until he's dead—far less so to most people to know that he has been put away out of conscience and out of mind in some place where he won't be seen or heard writhing in agony. My own feelings about this and other things, like being a vegetarian or going to see a bull-fight or following a hunt, are hopelessly mixed, but one thing I *know* is that I would never keep any creature in captivity in a cage, a hutch or—until I know more about it—in a goldfish bowl. The reason I take such pleasure in my bird-table is that all those who feed there, birds and squirrels, are free to come or go as they please, and that although they may be scared away by passers-by or unwonted noises, they know in the way that birds do, that no trap is set for them and no attempt will ever be made to restrict their liberty. The squirrels may scare the doves or even younger squirrels, the doves may scare the sparrows, the swallows may eat the gnats, but no intelligent being will offend any of them, and they know it, as they eat from my hands or go on eating while I pass the bird-table. I am disturbed but not distressed when I hear the park employees shooting pigeons or squirrels but I have nightmares when I remember small Moroccan boys selling trapped birds on strings by the roadside, or when I hear that in the past birds used to be blinded to make them sing more loudly.

Meanwhile, who are the visitors to my bird-table? First, naturally enough the sparrows, house sparrows, tree sparrows, and what we used to call hedge sparrows, which are in fact of a different species with sky-blue eggs and sharp beaks, and more correctly called dunnocks. I have been struck on closer acquaintance with the beauty of the plumage and colouring of all these birds, which are generally considered the plebs of the bird population of cities, even when one, *La Môme Piaf*, or simply Piaf, became the greatest cabaret and music-hall singer of her time. (Incidentally, she was the daughter of one of Oscar Wilde's protégés.) I am indignant at bird-watchers who affect to despise sparrows because they are, in both senses, common. They are endearing little creatures, and on a spring morning I listen attentively to 'the twittering of sparrows in the eaves', and I recommend the tints and patterns of the feathers to dress-designers.

The collared doves are almost as plentiful. They come from some giant conifers on the other side of the gardens and tennis courts which I overlook, and usually perch on one of those towering modern lamp-posts across the road, observing with their beady eyes before swooping down to the bird-table. I learn from a television film that the collared dove is in fact the one of the species most common in the Near East, so that it may have been the bird released from his Ark by Noah, and its wings may have been those of which I sang an anthem when I was in the choir of Tonbridge School chapel. The dove has been mentioned so frequently in English poetry, from Tennyson for whom it was burnished 'in the Spring', to Shakespeare for whom the female dove was 'patient' and Tennyson again for whom she 'moaned'. The popularity of the word in old-fashioned poetry may be accounted for by the fact that it provides almost the only rhyme to 'love'. But I think that does an injustice to the characterful creatures that sit staring at me from the railings in front of my window or peck so purposefully at the grain on the bird-table.

Only one jay has called here and he sat for barely a minute on the rail before going about his business. Seen at that range, he is a startling creature who shows the bright blue feathers over his wing-joints most noticeably. I knew these feathers long ago in Kent before I ever saw the bird itself, for I used to find them and collect them in a certain wood near Cage House. They are not more than two inches long; striped diagonally in blue and black, they give the whole bird a touch of brilliant contrast, and I know of no other British bird who displays that distinct blue. We get a number of blackbirds but frankly I value the male more for his glossy black feathers than for his infrequent whistling songs. Tennyson invokes him: 'O blackbird sing me something well!' but I hear more often his shriek in fright when he is disturbed than any sustained song.

The thrush is unfortunately a rarer visitor, though a welcome one. It would be pleasant to think that the larger missel-thrush derives its name from singing the Mass but the *Oxford Dictionary* disposes of any such romantic idea. 'Missel-toe', also spelt 'Mistle-toe', comes from the Old Norse 'Mistilteima' and has no connection with the Sacrament.

I think if I had to name my favourite among our birds (as we are fatuously asked to name our favourite books or composers or actors or colour or flowers), I would without hesitation say the blue tit, though the great tit and the coal tit run it close. I have not yet seen a bearded tit or a long-tailed tit, though I watch hopefully. The blue tit is flashy but not pretentious in colouring, courageous but not aggressive in character, intelligent but not greedy, wilful but not selfish. He thus has many of the qualities I most admire in a bird, and above all has an independence which makes him ignore attempts to bribe him with food, preferring to find his own and dart to it, then away with swift triumph. He is moreover a talented acrobat and will hang upside down by his claws as he picks at nuts over fine wire-netting. Altogether the most delightful bird who stays with us throughout the winter.

If it were only a question of colours, some of them quite exotic and brilliant in our sober English countryside, I suppose the chaffinch, greenfinch and bullfinch would be the most notable of ours in the garden lands of Bournemouth, though I daresay the goldfinch and yellowhammer —the first of which I have not seen—would be the most spectacular. Yellowhammers were common in Chipstead when I was a boy, so were wagtails both yellow and black-and-white, while magpies in groups of all sizes, promising the happiest omens, haunted the garden I overlooked in Ireland. Wrens come here fairly often but never stay more than a fleeting moment or two, while starlings are so damaging to the garden that they are the only birds I chase away.

Corn-buntings would embarrass me severely if they appeared for I know them under their culinary name of ortolans and have eaten them as Wilde did, 'wrapped in their Sicilian vine-leaves'. Occasionally a wood-pigeon who has a fierce but stupid expression in his stare strays up here from the public gardens, but since they are so plentifully fed by visitors there, they do no more than take a glance at our bird-seed before returning to the lawns below us.

No less welcome when they appear on most mornings except during the hardest of the winter are the many grey squirrels which come to eat the peanuts which we provide specially for them. That they are unshelled peanuts, or monkey-nuts as I prefer to call them, is explained by the fact that when shelled, the squirrels seize them before the birds have a chance to eat them. The doves are fond of swallowing them whole, so that I am alarmed at their digestion, while if I put them in a hanging box with fine netting across the bottom, the squirrels gnaw the box and get at them before the tits can peck at them. Trying to hang these feeding boxes out of reach of the squirrels is all in vain—they can climb or hang or twist themselves about till they achieve their object, which is amusing to watch but does not amuse the tits who are not fond of bird-seed and adore shelled monkey-nuts.

The squirrels have many curious habits and make friends with me most disarmingly. As they seldom live longer than the year in which they are born and do not come down to the patio before they are nearly full-sized, the time in which to coax them is all too brief, but generally serves to teach them to climb up to the window-sill and stare at me through the panes. I am frankly afraid to invite them into the room as their habits are mischievous and damaging to small objects or food that is lying about.

There is a certain amount of public hostility felt towards grey squirrels, chiefly for the illogical and unjust reason that they greatly outnumber the red ones whom they have all but displaced except in certain areas like the New Forest and the Forest of Arden—the Ardennes in fact—where they are still plentiful. But they are likeable creatures, fiercely defensive, watchful and humorous. It is their movements which are most pleasant to watch, when they sit upright with their tails curled up behind them, or when they run up and down posts or trees, or when they nibble impatiently at nuts held in their forepaws. They are altogether charming and with their huge bushy tails, totally unratlike. What I presume to be a male and a female will eat together on the bird-table but younger members of the same family, or at any rate species, who peep over the table edge at the food are promptly scared away, and have to wait till their elders have left. Their movements on the ground are also worth noticing—when hurried but not frightened, they have a kind of lightning waddle as they retreat. They also sit high on the apex of the thatched roof of the bird-table from which they seem to be watching in one direction, their dark oval-shaped eyes as motionless as their bodies till they abruptly change position to look somewhere else, frequently staring at me, not with hostility, I think, and certainly not with gratitude or affection, which would be unnatural and unpleasantly coy.

Shakespeare called the squirrel 'the fairies' coachmaker' —too fanciful a term perhaps for the lively and very real creature who is watching me at this moment. But he has a special charm for me; he is untidy and forgetful as I am. He carries unshelled nuts away in his mouth and hides them out of sight, though at no great distance, since he is back for more in a few seconds. That he subsequently forgets where the nuts were hidden is vouched for by W. H. Hudson, though he remarks that this forgetfulness is common to a great many animals and birds, including of course the domestic dog. I do not forget where food is hidden but with almost everything else, studs, pens, papers, handkerchiefs or shoes, I have frequently to appeal to Joseph, who has a gift for finding lost articles of all sorts. So I sympathize with the squirrel and dislike the English in India for calling their local squirrels, which are pretty little ring-tailed creatures, 'tree-rats'.

The amount of space I have in which to grow things is limited to a bed about twenty-two feet long and an average of two feet wide, and not more than a foot deep. Otherwise I have only giant cement-pots, troughs and smaller pots. But this suits me very well. Enough to experiment in a mild way, to change the bed with the seasons, to have pleasant surprises now and again and not too many disappointments.

I have been brought up among gardens, but as I realize now, when I can come to see and admit some of my father's weaknesses, he was what one may call not too unkindly a 'stockbroker gardener'. From Haxted House, Edenbridge, where I was born, to the Grange at Smarden in the Weald where he died thirty-five years later, he made a garden wherever we went, and his garden conformed to a pattern. There was always a tennis court, for long after he ceased to play himself, he laid out one for 'you children'. Once at Eastbourne he levelled off six feet of chalk to create a tennis court which we never had time to play on before my father discovered that the daily journey from town and a long bus ride afterwards was 'too much for him' and we moved to a flat in Warrior Square, St Leonards, where the gardens were public and had to be hired by the hour. The last tennis court he made was at New Barn in Kent, seven moves after Haxted House. But the tennis court was not the only invariable feature of my father's gardens. There was always a lawn with a magnificent herbaceous border, varying in richness according to my father's fortunes at the time from elaborate greenhouse-grown 'bedding-out plants' to less costly but always well selected annuals. Then some-where in the garden was what used to be called 'rustic work' with Dorothy Perkins roses spreading prolifically—too prolifically—over it. There was usually a rose garden and between the bushes a carpet of white alyssum with a border of lobelia. My father never worked in his gardens, but until his death in 1935, in bad times or good, he always managed to employ a gardener of some kind even when domestic servants were unobtainable. So when I looked at the narrow bed which runs in front of the railings of the patio I had some idea of what to do with it. Not that I should follow my father's plans to the letter even if there was space to do so. I had come to detest Dorothy Perkins as though she was a resented relative. And besides, I had made my own gardens, in Gloucestershire and Kent before the war, in India and in Sussex and above all in Tangier, where I had grown some things unusual even in that country of horticulture run riot.

But of course I had to adapt what knowledge I had to the limitations of my diminutive patch. It has taken three years to do so but now I have reasonable compromises to work on. The one long bed I crowd with spring bulbs, so thickly that they almost touch one another in the shallow compost-filled soil. At first I tried the conventional mixture of wall-flowers and forget-me-nots but I found two disadvantages. The wallflowers could not be obtained in a single colour and rust-coloured wallflowers mixed with yellow ones were really *too* much in the spirit of boastful little front gardens of terraced houses. Besides, the combination held up my planting of annuals with which I wanted to follow the bulbs to provide continuous colour seen from my windows. So they and the forget-me-nots have been dropped, not without regret, and I now have the long bed first over-crowded with daffodils, narcissus, hyacinths and tulips of contrasting but not shrieking colours and after that with annuals.

Along the end of the patio in the four large pots, I have four shrubs chosen from what a nurseryman had in stock, a camellia, a strawberry tree, an ornamental holly and a myrtle. The camellia buds strongly but rains damage the flowers with rust, though it promises a 'good year' each time round. Seven slightly smaller cement-pots have a variety of fuchsias which bloom with ardour for nearly six months. Pelargoniums fill the smaller pots, and gloxinias which I find rich and exotic. Over the railings, fighting for a foothold in the shallow bed, are climbing roses, clematis, clematis montana and honeysuckle, while somehow behind the bulbs are a number of prosperous chrysanthemums. Yet, believe it or not, I find space for experiments, often of plants which I grew in Tangier and which sometimes 'take' in this colder climate. I should add that between my patio and the road is a downward sloping bank on which *panticum* rhododendrons grow thickly and bloom with vigour. Being on the ground floor, my flat has French windows from my bedroom onto the patio, providing a covered space in which garden chairs stand ready for anyone who sees fit to contemplate the absurd little garden, so full of the colours of flowers and birds and the impudent staring eyes of squirrels. In the Summer I like to sit there watching the tennis players in the gardens below and enjoying the only drink my doctor thinks it wise for me to take—Scotch whisky and water.

Lameness has few advantages but among them is a licence to be lazy, while beautiful natural things are around one and one is consoled by the scent of summer flowers.

Thirteen

Midland Paradox

When I was a young man, I had a remedy in every crisis, every spell of boredom, every check in what I considered progress—it was to go abroad and look to my future for new experience. As I grow older I still look for experience, and call it adventure, but it is in the past I seek it, finding that to turn back and remember is more rewarding than to look forward to what may remain of my life, more full of surprises, lively encounters and nostalgic memories. I mean this literally, to use that much abused word. I like to travel, not to fresh woods and pastures new, but to places I have known and not visited for a long time, to renew friendships that have grown rusty while I was following my impulsive life. So that 'whan that Aprille with his shoures soote the droghte of March hath perced to the roote' and 'longen folk to goon on pilgrimages', I made up my mind to go back to the one region which had been the scene of the most formative years of my boyhood—the Midlands and the North. In *The Drums of Morning* I have recalled my days in that egregious school which was then called Wellington College, Salop, and is now known as Wrekin College, as closely if not as fondly as my years at Tonbridge School, but I had not visited the Wrekin or the school near its foot since leaving it in 1921. I decided to do so now, and asked and received permission from the present Headmaster to wander round the premises.

There were others in the ambiguous category of 'old friends' whom I would meet on this journey. I had kept in erratic touch with my school friend Malcolm Wolstenholme, a genuine eccentric with a tickling sense of humour in our schooldays, and a successful businessman with a charming wife, whom I had last seen in my years in the Cotswolds before the Second World War. I would meet him as I had done—could it be?—*forty* years ago in the downstairs bar of the Midland Hotel in Birmingham. There was also Donald Ebrahim, my doctor friend of slightly less, *three* decades ago in London, now in Coventry. There were also two hotels which I wanted to visit in Wellington, The Charlton Arms, to which my father and mother had taken me and my school friends to lunch during their visit to the school, and The Buck-a-Tree Hall which presumably had been enlarged from John Bayley's old home which I knew well.

Lastly there was the prospect of meeting another of my proudly miscellaneous collection of acquaintances, this time from a different period—an ex-matelot named Eric Bath who was one of the circle of servicemen who had had the freedom of my house at Ticehurst in the 1950s, as recounted in *The Life for Me*. I intended to make the journey north from the Brummagem area to meet him in Stockport where he had been given a one-room flat by the local authorities. Whatever he had lost in the intervening years from those days, he would have retained, I felt sure, the humour and Mancunian sense of independence which I remembered.

So altogether I longed to go on that pilgrimage, physically over the map and in spirit to the past, and chance whatever would befall me.

There was no question about my companion for this. Cynically it may be recalled that John Hitchcock had a car and could take a week away from his business, and had worked for some years in the Midlands himself. But these were not reasons in the spirit in which I made my plans. It was fitting and apt, I decided, that John, who had accompanied me in so many of those adventurous journeys abroad —to Normandy, the Rhineland, the Highlands, Switzerland and Morocco—would come with me this time. Although the particular revisits we should make would mean little or nothing to him, since we had met *only half a century ago* when I had left the Wrekin and all I had known there, he was willing to take me back. It was not easy for him to shift his business commitments to be free from May 19th to 26th, but he achieved it, and I spent the last week looking forward to our departure as though it were not to the Wrekin but to the Himalayas or the Pyrenees or Mount Athos.

It was a brilliant morning of sunshine and breeze when we set off in John Hitchcock's Volvo to find again, as I had done when I came to England three years ago, that the 'coloured counties' of the South at this time of year were translucent and lovely, rich with May blossom and the glory of flowering chestnut. It was a promising rather than an already fecund scene, spring having not quite passed to summer, and the edges of the road along which we sped uneventfully were white with cow-parsley. We drove north through Salisbury with her assertive spire, and turned towards the Cotswolds which I knew and loved well. When we stopped for lunch at the Cotswolds Gateway by Burford I remembered how, whenever with or without my brother Laurie I had driven from London to my little home in the village of Salperton, I had always stopped here and felt that it was indeed the gate to the Cotswolds, as Stirling was the gate to the Highlands.

These were, I felt as we drove on, the counties in which the Georgian poets had delighted, between Shakespeare's Warwickshire and Housman's Shropshire. These central counties were England itself, and though Kent was my particular birthplace, here in a no less nostalgic way I was at home among the grey stone walls.

But in the late afternoon we came into Shropshire itself, the county where my consciously developing boyhood had been spent. The red bricks and black beams of the houses in familiar villages welcomed me as they had done half a century ago and the names on signposts were recognizable as they had been when during that last glorious summer at school I had cycled out and explored Shrewsbury, Market Drayton, Shifnal and Lilleshall, or 'lovely little Lilleshall' as

172

I had called it in the bad Brookean verses I wrote then. We branched aside to pass the Ercall, the small sister of the great Wrekin which we could see from across the green levels, and I saw that the home of John Bayley, whose overpowering personality had dominated my teens as he dominated the school he had built, had indeed become 'The Buck-a-Tree Hall Hotel'. A far greater excitement to me was to find that the Tea Rooms at the foot of the Wrekin, which had provided me and my friends with 'Tuck', as we anachronistically called it, were standing unchanged and still called 'The Forest Glen Tea-Rooms'.

There was no way up the mountainside by which a car could reach the Halfway House or the summit—the pathway was sternly labelled 'For Pedestrians Only', at which I was rather relieved, having fears that tourist cars were now invited to ascend by the track which had seemed almost our own when we clambered higher and higher, chattering with Oswald Horrax of the 'Literature', 'Music' and 'Art' which absorbed us, as he and I had recalled in Durban during the last war when I ran that cheerful mentor to earth. I could not, of course, climb the Wrekin now but the rocky woodlands stretching up from the Forest Glen were evocative enough that May evening as I remembered so many visits to the mountain, oddly called 'Choir Outings', 'Whitmonday Holidays' or simply 'School Walks' from the anomalous Wellington College of long ago.

Then we drove into the market-town of Wellington and found that although it was not more changed than one would expect by the passage of time, it had now become embedded in the larger city of Telford, which spread its shopping streets and housing areas round the little Shropshire town I knew. But The Charlton Arms was in its heart, enlarged and modernised from the hostelry I remembered, in which my father and mother had stayed when they came to visit me. We drove round the school buildings, like the hotel enlarged and improved since 'my time' but recognizable with the eyes of nostalgic perception. I went to sleep that night hearing, at least in sentimental fancy, the voices of boys I had known, the 'boys who were boys when I was a boy', and reliving the only real hatred I have felt for another man in the whole of my life. Contempt, envy, ridicule, resentment—all these I have felt toward one or another of my fellows, but hatred, nurtured in boyhood and in memory till this day, only once and that for a schoolmaster named Dobson, a drunkard, a bully and—using the word with its precise Greek meaning—a pederast whom I described in *The Drums of Morning* and do not wish to recall again.

But I woke to more cheerful memories and ate against all my custom an 'English breakfast'. I was to meet the Head-master, Geoffrey Hadden, at mid-day, and when John Hitchcock had driven me up to Wrekin College I walked round the great red brick buildings I remembered to find the Headmaster's study where the Masters' Common Room had once been.

I soon realized what had happened to the quaint hybrid school I had known, modelled from the teachers' college imaginings of the magnificent John Bayley—it had become a great public school in the British tradition. The Governors to whom John Bayley had sold it had appointed as Head-master first Walker Maxwell Gordon, who had been a housemaster at Tonbridge when I was there, then the Rev. Guy Pentreath of Haileybury, then Robert Henry Dahl who had been an assistant housemaster at Harrow, and now Geoffrey Hadden from Charterhouse. None of them had been obediently conventional followers of the system they represented, but each was ambitious for Wrekin College and had pillaged the customs and histories of their previous schools to give it what they considered the best in life and traditions of its own. In this they had been successful, and I heard within an hour of entering the school from boys of the present regime of its victory at rugby football against the monster Manchester Grammar School and Denstone, of its achievements in study, cricket, swimming and shoot-ing, and I observed—something that cannot be faked by observer or observed—that the school's community was a happy one under a lively and resourceful Headmaster.

With somewhat morbid regret I might recall the 'big schoolroom', with classrooms round it having glass windows through which John Bayley could peer to see that the 'ma-a-sters' were doing their respective jobs, I might feel that 'Whitsun whole holidays' and school walks to the Wrekin were a loss, I might wonder whether any of the masters could instil the enthusiasm for English which Walter Howarth instilled, but I felt that if I was an Old Boy of Wrekin College I would be proud of it as—except in an amused and affectionate way—I had never been of 'Wellington College'.

This will not be understood by the promoters of education as it is practised in England today, the Labour Ministers and teachers who resent the whole public-school system and its products, who talk of snobbery and privilege and consider the schools which created generations of Colonial administrators as culpable as the colonies themselves. But in this, at least, I find myself with the minority, with Stalky and Tom Brown rather than with Mrs Castle and Billy Bunter and their language.

My schooldays were spent at two schools, three years to each—Tonbridge from 1914 to 1917, 'Wellington College, Salop' from 1917 to 1920. I found as I walked round the grounds of Wrekin College, that it was with Tonbridge that I felt the nearest affinity, however much among these shades of former years I recognized my own. And there was something altogether new to them both. The food was not only good but varied and well-presented. Conversation at the table at which I sat with the senior boys was more like the conversation in a university dining-hall than that among school juniors, and there was an air of good humour and responsibility about, as though the boys knew how to behave unself-consciously and with enjoyment of the passing hour.

That night we dined at Buck-a-Tree below the Ercall, and although the ghosts of past boyhood had crowded the college here, one ghost lived and reigned supreme, that of John Bayley himself. I have written of him in *The Drums of*

Morning and told how I knew him till his death in his hundredth year, but here in his home I saw him again, the square straight shoulders and the well-tailored clothes, the white waxed moustache, the fierce blue eyes that softened in after years to kindness, the whole forceful driving personality of the man. The dining-room in which we sat that evening looking over green fields to the giant outline of the Wrekin, the outline which John Bayley had seen for so many years. He had died twenty-four years before this date, failing to reach his hundredth birthday by only a few months. I repeated what I had written during his lifetime—'Whatever a Great Man is, John Bayley was one'.

Next morning we drove south to Birmingham. I am proud to have known, with a greater or less degree of intimacy, all four of the great centres of population in Britain, and of them I have spent the most time in the largest, Birmingham. This was because my schoolfellows in Shropshire came, most of them, from Brum, and because, as I recounted in *The Wild Hills*, I went to live for a time in John Hitchcock's rooms in Edgbaston. Then I had met every day with other friends in the downstairs bar of the Midland Hotel and remembered its customers as often 'theatricals', perhaps because one of The Co-Optimists of a few years before, Davey Burnaby, sat in a certain corner of it daily before lunch. Now that we were to spend a night in Birmingham I suggested this hotel for us and we had booked rooms there.

Each of those four cities had one of the great Victorian hotels, comfortable, a mite gloomy but prosperous-looking and well catered-for. However much new institutions may collect stars from the guidebooks, these remain solid centres of rich citizenship where 'business' is discussed at the Bar and in the Restaurant, in Birmingham at the Midland, in Glasgow at the Central, in Liverpool at the Adelphi and in Manchester at the Grand. So it was that now I was to meet Malcolm Wolstenholme, my friend at Wellington College, Salop, who came from Wolverhampton. I chose this place as the one of the many possible rendezvous most likely to arouse memories of the far past.

It worked. Malcolm was of my own age but so clearly resembled the sixteen-year-old I had known that I was startled and pleased to welcome him. I remembered him best for his dazzling sense of humour and his habit of rubbing his hands together in sheer glee under the desk when anything amused him. He had stayed with me in the school holidays in Eastbourne, lent me money when I had joined the Army as a private during the war, and sixty years later he could quote from irreverent verses of mine which I had composed in class.

So, old boys in both senses of the phrase, we talked of the Wrekin and John Bayley and the enthusiastic Walter Howarth, the loathsome Dobson and the mediocre Hammerton, of the Arts Club we had attempted to found after Horrax had put up a notice warning that 'No Philistines Need Apply', which had caused a number of sixth-form louts to mug me, under the pretence of taking prefectorial action probably deservedly, but quite unjustly. I told Malcolm to his septuagenarian amusement how the present Headmaster of Wrekin had told me good-humouredly that he would probably have expelled me for various exploits of mine in 1920 if our positions and ages had been reversed, and Malcolm showed me the photograph taken of the school gathered about John Bayley on the top of the Wrekin on Armistice Day 1918, in which we both figured. We rejoiced in the memory of the golf we had played on the school's links towards Hadley, and the port and pork pies we had enjoyed in the pub there while we were supposed to be playing Association Football.

I told Malcolm how impressed I had been by the school, but even more by the boys of the school as it was today, and we recalled old scandals and hostilities and a few small tragedies in our time. Our reminiscences lasted till the evening when John Hitchcock arrived from some metallurgical function he had attended and Malcolm left for Lapworth where he has lived ever since his marriage in the 1920s.

I can remember no happier or more worthwhile hours

than those spent among the young men of Wrekin College, and none which fulfilled so well the contradictory purpose of this chapter, to go back and forward at the same time. By the time we left Birmingham for Coventry to find two other symbols of my past and future, I was confused but happily interested.

My first object in Coventry was to discover the retreat of William Drakely who, as I have recounted in *The Licentious Soldiery*, had been at first the proverbial fear-inspiring Sergeant-Major of the Depôt Staff when I had joined the Intelligence Corps in 1940, and afterwards a good friend. Bill Drakely had been an N.C.O. in the Guards and afterwards a police officer before the war, but had been seconded to the 'I' Corps to do what he considered his function, to turn the pseudo-intellectual recruits in that heterogeneous unit into soldiers in three weeks. He took that job seriously, and I expected to find him taking his present job, owning a public house, if not as seriously, at least as successfully as his old one. It was soon evident that he did so. His customers were not drilled or disciplined as we had been in 1940 but evidently held the landlord and his wife and lovely young daughter in great affection. I remained gossiping with Bill Drakely for a hour and regretted that I could no longer challenge him to a trial on the dartboard, my right arm having failed me when my right leg did so.

I find few references in the books in this series to Donald Ebrahim, the doctor whom I should next visit in Coventry, which is strange, because in spite of a hiatus of the years between 1950 and 1973, he has been a close friend of both Joseph and myself. We met him just after the war when we were living in Doughty Street and he was a medical student. He is the son of Muslim Pakistanis, born in South Africa, and he married an English hospital nurse just after I knew him. She died in 1973, leaving him four splendid sons, Sharif, Rustum, Kim and Omar, whom I have met in rising order of age and increasing charm—Omar, then a chorister and schoolboy; Kim, always proudly characterized by his father as a 'rugby football player', though in fact a catering trainee; Rustum, a youth leader; and Sharif, a doctor. We found two of them, Rustum and Kim, with their father, whom they know as Don and treat as one of themselves.

This—as yet—all-male family seems to me unique in several respects, apart from its unusual origins. Its members discuss one another and their affairs (in both senses) with a freedom most communities would envy; Kim, it being agreed, was a traitor to the whole, having 'got himself engaged' to be married to a quiet and attractive girl. Sharif was an outsize intellectual like his father, who never reads a book unless it is a technical exposition of his own 'line'. Rustum brought in a friend who has a niche in this unusual family circle where everyone attempts to cap the last story or achieve a witticism considered memorable, like Omar's description of what should be the family's aim as 'Beige Power', rather than the Black Power of less hybrid citizens. Humour in fact rates high in the conversations of them all, as could be realized from the competitive chatter about us while we ate smoked salmon sandwiches made by Kim and drank Black Label whisky supplied by Don.

The hour that followed was as delightful as any in that nostalgic week, one of those occasions when I realize that the rewards of maintaining old friendships and adding to them as they multiply pay dividends, even now when I cannot undertake wide-ranging distances in travel or embark on more passionate adventures in relationships. All these young men, among whom I include Donald for all his advanced degrees in medicine and psychiatry, have a responsiveness, an attraction, a humour and a lovability which is found all too rarely in my adolescent friends, and I feel privileged to be accepted so generously among them.

They have the gift of making swift decisions in which they all concur without fuss or small selfish disagreements, and when John and I told them that we had booked our room in an Esso hotel off the M5 motorway and near Bill Drakely's pub, they all agreed to follow us there. This 'Esso Hotel' was a curious caravanserai, covering a large acreage in motel fashion, with a dance-floor, bars, restaurants and vast car-parks, as one would expect from its name and purpose. Don had hired a taxi so that he would not have to drive home after we had remained unconfined (though as it happened moderate) in our drinking among the massed motorists of this place. Good talk again, and I felt young and forgot my lameness and was content. Youth always inspires me.

On our way next morning (Sunday) somewhere between Coventry and Stockport—I am no topographer—we passed through the little town of Wilmslow, which like another 'little town' in Cheshire was the fictional abode of the Misses Matilda and Mattie Jenkyns, daughters of the Rector. I did not stop in Knutsford to find whether there remain any vestiges of that remarkable woman Elizabeth Gaskell who wrote so much more than *Cranford*, but stopped outside number 31 Manchester Road, Wilmslow, which I knew was the antique shop of my friend Norman Trace, with whom during my years in the Cotswolds I had enjoyed picaresque forays into the antiquarian book and antique trade.

We had shared a shop in Cheltenham and I taught Norman Trace all I knew of antiquarian bookselling, and he in return gave me rather more generously much of his considerable knowledge of furniture, paintings, porcelain, pottery, bronze, silver and watercolours. No one could blame us when, thanks to this knowledge, I bought in open auction a watercolour by 'Michaelangelo' Rooker for three pounds which, after it had travelled with me over thousands of miles abroad and through four decades of time, I sold through Christie's for a thousand guineas. Or when I gambled on the fact that none of the other booksellers in the Midlands would know that Samuel ('*Erewhon*') Butler, had written a book trying to prove that Homer was a woman so that I was able to attend a remote sale in the country to purchase this unadvertised rarity for a few shillings. Or when we had both collaborated in taking advantage of esoteric knowledge gained in the past to make our business thrive.

When we called at Norman's address that Sunday

morning, the shop was closed and we had to telephone from a pub to bring him out. But he came, seeming little older than he had been when I met him in Manchester to consult him on details necessary in my novel *Brass Farthing* nearly thirty years since, and we shocked John Hitchcock by recalling our opportunist dealings long ago.

Norman's shop was for sale and he would, he said, in future deal only rarely from a private house or flat where he would not be persuaded into addressing the Women's Institute of the place on '*The Collection and Valuing of Antiques*'. Like me he was 'getting on' into his seventies, but unlike me he was able to retire from the rat-race. He was as cheerful and informative as ever, and we recalled old brushes with the booktrade, sometimes hilariously. John, who inherited from his Puritan forebears a passion for the smallest scruples of honesty, was not greatly amused.

Of all that I had seen then or at any time of the Industrial North, the Midlands, the Black Country and the rest of those regions with forbidding names and slummy areas, I was promised that Stockport would be the blackest and grimmest, and I welcomed this because, as I realized that Sunday morning, I had never been in one of the tower blocks or built-up areas attached to a great city of factories or mines, and I knew that my friend Eric Bath, whom I was to visit, lived in just such a home in just such a suburb of just such a town. The last time I had seen anything like it was in the thirties when I had gone with some of the Rosaires to visit someone in Hull, and seen the Sunday noontime garbage left in the streets by Saturday-night crowds, and smelt the dinners cooking in thousands of close-packed proletarian homes. Evidently if I was to claim to have seen England as it is in the 1970s I ought to know something of a life, near in distance but far in style from the green and luscious counties through which we had passed, and Stockport, John promised me, would satisfy some at least of my impudent curiosity.

But at first it did not. The centre of the town through which we passed was spaced and dignified with no sign of slums or smoke, with such buildings as courthouse, chapel, Town Hall and cinema drawing attention to themselves. Eric lived in an authentic tower block, not constructed for television comedy, but populously inhabited. Three of these monsters rose to an imposing height in the Stockport suburb of Brinnington, and on the second—or was it third or fifth or tenth floor of one of these?—'Ludlow Towers', Eric had been leased a flat by the Housing Department of Stockport to compensate him for the destruction of his late parents' home by the Planning Department. Perhaps it was also in recognition of his thirty years of unblemished record in the Royal Navy and Merchant Service. At all events, he lived here alone, in the intervals between his stays in psychiatric hospitals and homes.

A score of children played noisily among the cars standing in the large park of the building, clean and well-dressed children, shouting Mancunian jeers to one another. A five-year-old boy who spoke not a word in answer to my query for Eric's flat took up a child's tricycle and led me through the bare front entry-hall to the lift. My silent cicerone made his way to this, expertly set the lift in motion and, when it had risen to the right floor, pushed his vehicle out to the landing, where a party-door divided a set of flats from the main building. He rang the bell of one of the nearest of them, then totally ignoring my amused thanks, went as he came without a word, symbol, I decided, of the place and its people, friendly, uninquisitive and noisy.

Eric was not in but the inevitable kindly neighbour from the flat opposite gave me information.

'I expect he's gone round to The Cheshire Cat for a game of darts,' she said. 'He usually does on Sunday morning. He's only been gone half-an-hour but I don't expect he'll be long.'

The Cheshire Cat was the pub I had noticed at the corner of the road, and as it was now two o'clock and mid-day closing time, I was relieved to see Eric appearing from the lift.

He had changed, of course. It was twenty-five years since

I had seen him in Ticehurst, and he had suffered a major operation and several break-downs since then. Moreover his speech had lost its pronounced Lancashire accent, so that he pronounced book as book and not boo-ook. He told me later that he had been hurt when I pulled his leg about this. He had also lost his bright blond hair and cheery matelot manner but the large shining blue eyes and the satirical twist of his lips were still there. All this interested me. He was alone in the world, all his relations (save one septuagenarian sister) were dead and he was living on a small Government allowance. He had no friends, having been isolated from his acquaintances in the Andrew and what he called the 'Merch' by his long periods in hospital. He was approaching fifty years old now, a sad, lonely man, not self-pitying but lacking much zest for living.

His flat of two rooms, a bedroom and minute kitchen, was scrupulously clean and tidy, as the flat of a naval man might be expected to be. He had inherited it two or three months ago from a family who had left him with a lot of cleaning up to do.

I suppose he was an example of the drop-out of our times, provided for adequately, given quarters and sufficient money to buy enough to eat, able to read books from the public library and obtain medical advice from the 'National Health', kept alive in other words, and allowed as much freedom as was thought good for him. He did not grumble —his attitude was fatalistic and not ungrateful. He was the very type for whom the Welfare State had been created.

He spoke nostalgically of his visits to Ticehurst and flatteringly remembered many things I had said and done there, so that he revived in me much of the carefree spirit of those happy days. He had kept copies of my books during all the years since 1953 when we both had travelled widely, and had read a surprising number more. I was pleased that I had come to meet him again now, and did what I could to make his life more interesting and his surroundings less arid.

Next morning John turned the Volvo southward and we started on the long journey home.

Fourteen

A Death and a Life

It chanced that in one Summer day (5th June, 1976) there were two events which pointed up both the spring and autumn, the setting out and closing in of the life through which I am passing, for on that day I heard of the death at seventy-one of Patrick, Lord Kinross, most dear, staunch and generous of my friends, and I met the sprite Simon, the seven-year-old son of my nephew and godson, Derek. So mortality and infancy greeted one another over my head.

The loss of Patrick Kinross was to me paralysing, as I daresay it was to many others, for he had a genius for friendship and had been to many men and women their most loved contemporary. To me I think he was more, for ever since the day in 1953 when he had come to my rescue in a crisis, he had been counsellor and giver of aid and encouragement to me, besides perennially my host, some-times for weeks at a time, in his house in Little Venice when-ever I had come to London. He had collected and reviewed my books and through him I had made a number of friends and from him I had learnt all I know of the Levant. Three years ago he had for a time abandoned the comfortable house which he found harder each year to leave to come across Belgium to my seventieth birthday party in the Rhineland, for it amused him that I should be celebrating it with a large circle of my friends in the village in which I had written my first novel forty years earlier. Last year I had dined with him and Crystal Hale in his pleasant base-ment dining-room. Monty Compton Mackenzie had been a beloved character to both him and me, a source of fre-quent conversation and humour. Patrick had stayed with me in Sussex and Tangier and had laughed with me over the eccentricities of many people in public life and out of it. Frankly I felt doubtful as to whether I could patch up my life now that his death had broken it down, and I resolved never to go near the house in Little Venice which had been as a home to me. I sent flowers to his funeral but could not attend it in company with his countless friends, especially when I learnt from an evening newspaper that Patrick had made a suggestion to his friend and mine, John Betjeman, to arrange a party for all Patrick's friends and in his home after the funeral. Only the death of Patrick's fellow Wykehamist Bosie Douglas thirty-three years ago had hit me so hard.

Patrick's home in Little Venice was as familiar to me as any of my own homes from 1954 to 1974. I had lived in it for stays of a week to three months when I had come to London from Tangier or from other places in which I had settled. It was difficult indeed to realize that I should not again arrive on its doorstep with my bags and a supply of whisky (which was cheaper in Morocco than in Scotland) to hear from Patrick which of his two guest bedrooms I was to occupy and at what time he nowadays had his break-fast of toast, Cooper's Oxford Marmalade and coffee, at which we growled greetings but rarely exchanged anything but the barest threads of conversation. I know his habits well—how he would rise from the breakfast-table in the basement and shut himself in his sitting-room overlooking the canal. He would work, and unwillingly but amicably answer 'phone calls and write off brief letters to satisfy his many correspondents, then leave the house for the walk in Regent's Park which occupied him till tea-time. In the evening his friends would call, either for a drink or to dine when Patrick had cooked one of the imaginative dinners to which he liked inviting them. He preferred doing this to dining out in a restaurant or at the Travellers' Club, and (especially of late) he rarely broke his pleasant routine. Once a year or so he would go abroad—often to Turkey which was a second homeland to him, giving him a royal reception whenever he went to Ankara—but he had ceased leaving his home for weekends in country houses, saying that he preferred his own friends and fireside to most entertainment.

His obituary in *The Times* on June 7th did justice to him as a man and as a writer.

'From 1953 to 1957 he was associated with *Punch*, then under the editorship of his friend Malcolm Muggeridge, and a visit to the United States for *Punch* provided the material for *The Innocents at Home* (1959).

'Meanwhile repeated visits to Turkey led to a deepening interest in Turkish history. This found expression in a notable biography of Ataturk (1964). Since the Ataturk papers were inaccessible in the vaults of the Ottoman Bank, it was based largely on first-hand information from surviving colleagues and personal friends. *Between Two Seas* (1968) was written to mark the centenary of the Suez Canal, but soon after, reverting to the country of his preference, he embarked on the long study for another book, entitled *The Ottoman Centuries*, of which the manuscript had been sent to the printers at the time of his death.

'As a result of his writings, and his close acquaintance with the remoter parts of the country, Kinross came to enjoy a reputation in Turkey that was unique for an Englishman. A young curator at the Bodrum Museum who said: "Greece has her Lord Byron, but now Turkey has her Lord Kinross", was expressing more than a half truth.

'Though his life of Ataturk was highly professional, it is perhaps as a traveller-writer that Kinross will be remembered. His books of travel, the product of sympathy, observation, wit, and an unconventional mind, reveal unusual powers of evocation and description. They have their own flavour and can stand beside the best of their time.

'As a man Kinross never ceased to develop. From the acid columnist emerged the perceptive traveller and dedicated writer. Years increased his understanding and the range of his sympathies, and his appearance came to recall that of a splendid but benevolent Old Testament prophet. With loyalty and a rich talent for friendship, he had an unusually wide circle of friends, and many who dined at his house in Warwick Avenue appreciated the significance of the entry in *Who's Who*: "Recreation—cooking". With interests undiminished, he retained a passion for work until his final illness.'*

No, I decided as I wrote about Patrick in the week after his death, No, I would not go to his funeral or attend the kind of Wake which John Betjeman was organizing in the house in Little Venice. Except for John himself and Crystal Hale, Patrick's friends were not mine and I should only feel embarrassed by the sight of them being dutifully cheerful as Patrick had wished them to be. I mourned him and could not pretend to anything else.

To my great-nephew, as I suppose I must call Simon, though it is a ponderous name for such a lively and radiant little boy, I can only be grateful for his arrival in my life at the moment of this loss from the far end of experience. I saw him first below the bank and across the road where he stood cheerfully waving his hand to me, an unknown uncle to whom he was being taken for a visit. I remembered my own hostility at his age towards the uncles I had known and was cheered to find that at least he viewed me without unfriendly preconceptions. My freakish ability to recall the events and acquaintances of my early childhood makes me wary of powers of recollection in small children, knowing that a snub or reproof may rankle for years in growing minds. As I avoided 'talking down' to the less erudite of my fellow soldiers during the war, so I have learned to hold conversations with my juniors as between two grown men; never to patronize, tease, nor deride, however amiably, the little boys and girls who are good enough to accept me as one of themselves. There are a number of these, the children of my friend Clifford Gibbs, of my cousin Stephen Oliver, the little son whom I am describing of my nephew and god-son Derek Cooke and more, as they say, to come. With all of these there is an understanding, I like to think, by which I

* By permission of *The Times*.

187

do not play the grown-up to them and they do not too remotely behave with awe, or distance or respect to me.

It was quite evident in the first moments of my meeting with Simon that he was instinctively following the attitude of my other small friends. He was a singularly beautiful little boy, with thick blond hair and thoughtful eyes inherited from his young father. When I remembered the stiff garments I had to wear at his age, Eton suits and starched collars, I found that his breezy clothes, bare legs and open neck looked refreshing and free. He talked quietly but with occasional scraps of knowledge surprising in view of his age. Thus when I was clumsy enough to start explaining what a pseudonym was, he suggested that it was 'like Mark Twain', and he read out pieces of a book of mine with expression and lucidity. Most rewarding of all, and most pleasing to my vanity, was that he evidently 'took to' me, spoke to me man to man and instantly nudged his way into my life in a manner that would make it difficult if not impossible to eradicate. I had, in fact, achieved a relationship with my little great-nephew, and only an elderly fellow-bachelor will quite understand how precious this was to me.

It was also welcomed by both his father and mother, with whom Simon was apt to do what is called in the language of adults 'get his own way'. They were both proud of him, as well they might be, but did not—again in that peculiar vocabulary used by grown-ups discussing children—'spoil' him, or at least not more than was 'good for' him. He was guilty occasionally of funny little rebellious acts, not of 'naughtiness' but of humorous mischief. He was not, in other words, cherubic or saintly in a Victorian way but enjoyed his carefree young life. And in his eyes there was not the least shadow of the prison-house closing about him.

It is still Saturday, 10th June, as I write these words, proof that I have at last caught up and for the first time write as events take place, having come towards the very end of the book I set out to write on a morning twenty years ago in Tangier. As I do so 'The End' eludes me and I begin to realize that there is no end. The brave determination I had

when I began to tell the whole story of a life in this twentieth century from which light could be flashed down on
the century itself, fails to be complete because there is no
such thing as completion. Even as I turn back to read
earlier passages of clearly remembered incidents, others
spring into place and other beings enact them. Melodies
are heard and scents arise which I failed to describe and
though I come towards the last of twenty-four books and
two million words, I could fill another dozen at least with
material from the same source. The most I can hope of all
this wordage is that to a social historian of the future it may
tell in words and not through the less vital media of film
or television or any future invention, something of the life
of an Englishman who sought for adventure and did not
wait for it to come to him, who enjoyed every passing
episode, whose gusto never failed and whose attitude to his
fellows rarely led him to feel contempt or boredom.

Who, moreover, has always looked ahead, and does so
now even though there are diminishing sunsets in view.
Not for me a long regretful *vale* or frightened realization
that night is falling, since however few the years ahead they
will be busy and fruitful. The writing of this long series of
books is finished but I have yet to prepare it for publication
as a series, finding and naming the illustrations which I hope
may one day embellish its pages, correcting the errors and
adding, here and there, to the incidents—enough work to
occupy many happy days. I have yet to make more friends
and possibly write another book or two. For one thing is
certain—I shall never be able to stop writing. It is not,
perhaps, the most giddily happy fate to be born mouthing
phrases, but it is an irreversible one. I shall write so long as
I still have something to say, narrative, argument or poetry,
and so long as I can still find someone to listen to me. A
threat, perhaps? Certainly a promise. Writing—and I mean
the actual movement of pen over paper as well as the effort
of composition—is for me not a diversion, a means of
earning a living, or an art, it is a necessity as I discovered
when I was recovering from the stroke which deprived me

for a while of the ability to practise it. Well or badly, I must write, and welcome every day which brings to me a new supply of folio lined pages in the pattern I have used since boyhood, fairly thick and not too smooth.

To vary this occupation, the round of the seasons is enough for me, mornings of winter when Jack Frost has breathed on my window, the rousing bird life of spring, the transient days of the English summer and the glorious plenty of autumn, all of them inviting me to write, to string more words together, to ponder over new turns of phrase or the noise of a finale, to write as I did behind a desk-lid in school or secretly after bed-time, or lying on the green, green grass of home. I have demanded no recognition and very little reward, but have been satisfied that in each change of circumstance and whatever the demands, I have persisted in writing as well as I can, so that I may say of this book and each of my books that however it may be abused, it is the best of which I am capable. For to offer anything less to those few faithful readers who borrow my books from lending libraries would seem to me the cardinal sin of any writer.

Looking back on the volume of my work I recognize that there is far too much of it, but I am not sure that if I had written less I should have written better, or that any writer would have done so. Notoriously prolific writers like Balzac or Edgar Wallace almost certainly would not, in their separate styles, have done so. Each one writes at his natural pace, thinking and creating in time with the progress of his pen or dictaphone, and I do not believe he can do otherwise successfully.

This may also be true of the typing of books or letters or articles. I calculate that since the time when he rashly threw in his lot with mine, Joseph has typed twenty of my own novels, twenty-five novels published under a pen-name, thirty non-fiction books of mine, each of them averaging eighty thousand words in length, as well as all the correspondence occasioned by these or my private life, in addition to articles, short stories scraps of verse and prose, and file upon file of other material. Yet he has never rushed this work to its detriment, and each letter, each page of typescript, has shown that he is a perfectionist. Although for the business-like reason that Joseph took no very large part in literary creation he does not formally rank as my collaborator, yet if his has not been collaboration what has it been? When the mendacious Paul Lund, whose criminal life-story I wrote in *Smiling Damned Villain*, reported to the circle of friends in his Tangier bar: 'Rupert doesn't write. The 'Indu does it all for him' he was nearer than he meant to be to the truth (though characteristically inaccurate in the matter of Joseph's religion).

Joseph's devotion to my work may be reason enough for dedicating, as I intend to, the whole book *The Sensual World* to him. But other obligations cannot be acknowledged in this way. Joseph has suffered poverty and imprisonment, disparagement and unpopularity through his loyalty to me, has nursed me through illnesses and protected me from fraud, and only rarely has shared in what small portion of triumph I have known. There is no form of repayment for these, certainly not the too easily expressed one of a dedication. Those tricksy lines opening with someone's name and 'But for whom . . .' or 'But for whose . . .' after it, look trivial on the dedication page when they seek to express gratitude for all the thirty years I owe to Joseph.

I cannot look back on the achievement of the twenty-four volumes of this sequence with the satisfaction of having done all I set out to do, for I am perpetually remembering events for which I should have found a place. I am rather like a greedy small boy who wants everything for himself and regrets this or that sweetie of description or familiarity which he has not crammed in his mouth. Perhaps above all I regret that I have not found as a writer one area of the world (and particularly of Britain) of which I can say 'this is my own, my native land'. There have been many places, as this book testifies, for which I feel nostalgia, even more literally homesickness, but I have not remained in them long enough to appropriate them in the books I have written. Hardy's Wessex, Bennett's Potteries, Scott's Lowlands,

Gaskell's Cranford, Kingsley's Devon, or the Lake District, East Anglia, Wales, Liverpool, Manchester or the Cotswolds, which have been the literary stamping-grounds of various writers, have been for me no more than places affectionately visited, or revisited in this last book of the series. For I have been, and am proud to have been, a nomad, my homes no more than the camping-sites of a gypsy, and my writings little better than snapshots taken with some little experience in view-finding. At least it is as a true Romani that I have travelled, not as one of the sentimentally conceived 'travelling folk' and didakais of popular fiction. At least my snapshots are my own and owe little to other more skilled photographers.

Perhaps it is more by luck than judgement that the record stretches very far across the century, from the year 1903 when I was born to 1976 when I finish, so that I clearly remember if not the very first motorcars at least the first to belong to any of my family or be a common sight on the roads, and that among public events I recall blazoned in headlines or discussed by my elders was the sinking of the *Titanic*, the death of General Booth of the Salvation Army ('Wonderful old fellow' my father said), the tragedy of the Captain Scott Expedition, the first aeroplanes to cross the Channel which I watched from Banstead Downs, the death of Edward VII, for whom the boys of my preparatory school wore black bands on their straw hats, the public abuse of Lloyd George among the Conservatives who were my father's friends, and the gradual replacement by unreliable taxis of the hansom cabs we knew. From these my memory is more continuous down to the sensational and heroic rescue of Israeli hostages by their own Commandos from more than a thousand miles away.

So now lest I continue worrying at this book, let me write a word in bold letters across its page and post the manuscript unrevised to my publisher, who must bear some responsibility for encouraging me to complete it.—

FINIS